For all the generations of Chevy truck owners who have made possible
100 Years of Building the Future.

Brimming with creative inspiration, how-to projects, and useful information to enrich your everyday life, Quarto Knows is a favorite destination for those pursuing their interests and passions. Visit our site and dig deeper with our books into your area of interest: Quarto Creates, Quarto Cooks, Quarto Homes, Quarto Lives, Quarto Drives, Quarto Explores, Quarto Gifts, or Quarto Kids.

Inspiring | Educating | Creating | Entertaining

This edition published in 2019 by Crestline,
an imprint of The Quarto Group
142 West 36th Street, 4th Floor
New York, NY 10018 USA
T (212) 779-4972 F (212) 779-6058
www.QuartoKnows.com

First published in 2017 by Motorbooks, an imprint of The Quarto Group,
100 Cummings Center Suite 265D, Beverly, MA 01915, USA.

Crestline titles are also available at discount for retail, wholesale, promotional, and bulk purchase. For details, contact the Special Sales Manager by email at specialsales@quarto.com or by mail at The Quarto Group, Attn: Special Sales Manager, 100 Cummings Center Suite 265D, Beverly, MA 01915, USA.

10 9 8 7 6 5 4 3 2 1

ISBN: 978-0-7858-3747-3

Acquiring Editor: Zack Miller
Project Manager: Alyssa Bluhm
Art Director: Brad Springer
Cover Designer: Commonwealth // McCann
Layout: Silverglass Design

Printed in China

General Motors Trademarks used under license to Quarto Publishing Group USA Inc.

GM
OFFICIAL
LICENSED PRODUCT
99-6602-34417

Chevrolet
Trucks

100 YEARS
OF BUILDING THE FUTURE

CRESTLINE

Contents

Foreword

To me, the benefit of any history book is the perspective it provides for today, and tomorrow.

Reading Larry Edsall's review of the first hundred years of our truck production is no exception. While navigating the many generations, models, and changes that are inevitable over a century, some patterns emerge that help explain the enduring legacy of Chevy Trucks.

For example, our most iconic trucks were created to fit a specific customer need. The very first Chevrolet trucks were built as parts runners for the factory. We introduced our first fleetside truck bed in 1955 for customers who wanted more cargo room. We introduced our first dual-rear wheel truck in 1973 for customers who wanted more payload capacity.

As a result, Chevrolet has offered a wide variety of choices for truck buyers over the past hundred years. For the reveal of the 1947 "Advance Design" trucks, Chevrolet featured ninety-nine different body configurations on nine wheelbases! This stemmed from the realization that truck customers are too diverse for a "one size fits most" approach. Cattle ranchers and weekend campers both buy trucks, but they need very different trucks for very different uses.

Finally, it is apparent that from the very first trucks Chevrolet built that we understood durability is paramount for truck buyers. People buy trucks to work—whether that work is hauling parts in an assembly plant, transporting a crew of ranch hands, or towing a camper on summer vacation. That focus was evident when Chevrolet drove a half-ton truck, carrying a half ton of weight, ten thousand miles across the United States with no repairs—an incredible feat in 1937.

These patterns are still true today. Chevrolet continues to build trucks tailor-made for different customers, with a three-truck strategy compromised of the Colorado, Silverado 1500, and Silverado HD. We continue to offer customers a wide variety of truck choices, from the agility of the Colorado ZR2 off-road truck to the towing confidence of the Silverado 3500 HD, with a staggering 445 horsepower and 910 pound-feet of torque. Most importantly, we continue to design, engineer, and build each truck with the goal of offering unrivaled durability, which is why Silverado remains the most dependable, longest-lasting full-size trucks on the road.

Looking forward, we are confident these patterns will continue to influence Chevy Trucks for the next hundred years.

We hope you enjoy this book, and thank you for your continued support of Chevrolet.

Best,
Alan Batey
Global Head of Chevrolet

Introduction

From the beginning, Chevrolet trucks have been designed to meet customer needs and enhance customer lifestyles, whether that involved those working in the trades, fighting a war, or, more recently, towing trailers for weekend recreation. In many cases, features on Chevrolet pickups were rolled out even before customers realized they needed them—something the auto industry calls "surprise and delight."

But this may be the most delightful surprise I discovered while researching this book: because they needed a specialized vehicle to move parts around within their assembly plant, Chevrolet staffers were building trucks for their own use two years before Chevy trucks were offered for sale to consumers.

These earlier half-ton trucks built in 1917 were based on Chevrolet's 490 model passenger car, though with the rear bodywork replaced by a platform for hauling parts and parcels around the plant.

There was a need—and they found a solution. Soon there would be loyal customers from coast to coast and beyond, people devoted to their Chevy trucks. They weren't about to look at another brand the next time they were in the market for a new truck.

Those Chevrolet trucks met customer needs, and they did it while also fulfilling what would become the legacy of Chevy trucks: they proved themselves to be "the most dependable, longest-lasting" pickups on the road.

Chevrolet's First Trucks

Ever since the first Chevrolet truck rolled off an assembly line a hundred years ago, those trucks have been designed, engineered, and built to meet one primary mission: to enhance the owner's life, whether it be at work or, increasingly as modern lifestyles evolved, at leisure activities.

Think of the challenge involved in building such diverse capabilities in a single vehicle, to provide a purposeful *and* practical vehicle while also offering the needed flexibility of service across the spectrum of truck owner demands.

From the start, one of the most challenging tasks for Chevrolet's engineers and designers has been fulfilling the customer's present wants while identifying the customer's future needs, even before he or she had recognized those needs.

It's been that way throughout the hundred-year history of the Chevrolet pickup truck. In fact, it was that way for a couple of years *even before* there was a Chevrolet truck.

Although that first Chevy truck wasn't produced until January 1918, the need for such a versatile, capable vehicle was clear to those working at Chevrolet assembly plants. Because of this need, they took a few Chevrolet passenger cars, reinforced the load-carrying components, removed some of the rear body panels, and replaced them

with platforms to carry parts and supplies. *Voilà!* The Chevrolet truck was born and, initially, put into service ferrying various parts from place to place at the company's assembly plants.

Maybe it was the sight of such vehicles and their effectiveness at meeting the chores at hand that led Chevrolet executives to approve the production of their own—and official—truck models. The role of trucks pressed into service with troops fighting in World War I may have been another factor.

It was in January 1918, just a few months before Chevrolet became part of General Motors, that Chevrolet's first series-produced trucks, designated as the Model T, appeared.

Those first trucks were open-cab vehicles using the same cowls and flat, but rear-slanting, windshields as Chevrolet's cloth-topped, open-sided passenger cars. Standard equipment included a speedometer, ammeter, tire pump, electric horn, and twelve-spoke hickory-wood wheels with demountable rims, as well as other essentials.

OPPOSITE: A 1916 Chevrolet 490 passenger car, converted into the configuration that would have been used in a Chevrolet assembly plant up to two years before the company produced trucks for commercial sales. *Vintage Chevrolet Club of America*

Chevrolet based its first trucks on its 490 passenger car chassis, such as this 1918 touring version appearing in a classic car show.

Chevrolet's overhead-valve inline four-cylinder provided motivation, but with modifications to provide more displacement via a longer stroke and more power—37 horsepower compared to 26 for the passenger car version.

Customers bought the rolling chassis (manufacturer's suggested retail price: $595) and worked with dealers or aftermarket suppliers to secure whatever bodywork was required for their specific needs.

In addition to Light Duty trucks, the Model T also was available in three heavy-duty versions:

Worm-drive chassis, $1,325
Flare Board Express truck, $1,460
Curtain Top Express, $1,545

In its January 19, 1918, edition, the automotive trade magazine *Automobile Topics* proclaimed in a two-deck headline that such a truck would be coming before the end of the calendar year:

Chevrolet Reveals One-ton Truck With
Capacious Canopy-top Body
Has Valve-in-head Unit Power Plant and
Worm Drive—Speed Limited by Governor—
Wheelbase 125 Inches

"Regular equipment includes a flareboard body with canopy top on eight substantial supports, and side curtains," the report noted. "The driver is protected by a windshield. The top can be removed by releasing the stanchions where they fasten to the body sills. The loading space is 114½ inches long, 45¾ inches wide and the depth of the body is 14¼ inches."

In a shorter article, *Motor Record* headlined its report:

New Chevrolet Truck Shows Careful Design

Soon, a Light Delivery truck based more closely on the 490 passenger car was added to the truck line. While the 490 numbers continued to be counted in the car category, Model T production soared to 6,098 units in 1919, with trucks coming off assembly lines in Flint, Michigan; Tarrytown, New York; St. Louis, Missouri; and Oakland, California.

"The popularity of Chevrolet trucks was starting to rise," *The Standard Encyclopedia of American Light-Duty Trucks* notes in its entry detailing the 1919 model year. It also indicates that, while the 490 truck was a carryover vehicle in its second year, the medium-/heavy-duty Model T truck benefited from Chevrolet's FB engine.

By 1919, Chevrolet Model T medium-/heavy-duty trucks were being produced in Bay City and Saginaw, Michigan, as well as in Flint; in St. Louis; Tarrytown; Oakland; Fort Worth, Texas; Toledo, Ohio; and Oshawa, Ontario, Canada.

In the "Instructions for Operation and Care of Chevrolet Model 'T' One Ton Worm-Drive Motor Truck," owners were reminded that the "hardest of all operation rules to remember and observe" was **Do Not Overload.**

The evils of overloading are understood by most users of motor trucks but there are many times when they do not make use of this knowledge.

The Chevrolet truck is built so well that it can be overloaded without any apparent noticeable depreciation—but there is depreciation even though it does not seem to be noticeable.

Tires, bearings, differential, worm, wheels and, in fact, every part of the truck is affected by the overload and time will show the effects.

Loads should be watched carefully because the life of your truck as well as your repair expense will largely depend upon it.

Little did the writers of this owner's manual know that Chevrolet's trucks proved so strong and steadfast that they became the most dependable, longest-lasting trucks on the American road.

Although Chevrolet still didn't produce what we would recognize as pickup bodies for its trucks, in 1920 it equipped the 490 line with fully crowned fenders and headlamps mounted on the front fenders instead of the former tie-bar setup. The company also

Remove the bodywork from the cowl rearward on a Chevrolet 490 passenger car and you have the basis for Chevy's first series of trucks.

The Chevrolet 490 Sedan as an Open Car for Touring in Pleasant Weather. The Price Is $1,060

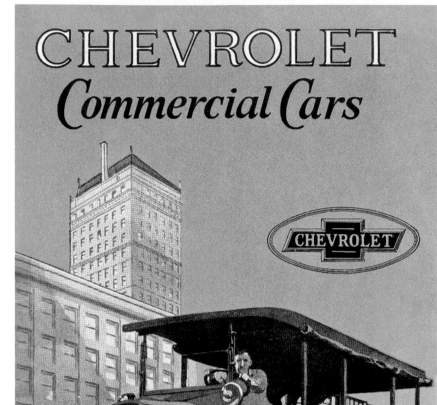

CHEVROLET
Commercial Cars

CHEVROLET

One Ton Truck

An early sales brochure referring to Chevrolet's first trucks as "Commercial Cars."

bodywork, as well as a "farm wagon" setup for showcasing fresh produce at the marketplace.

Meanwhile, the Model T one-ton truck was shown with passenger bus, fire truck, wholesale hauling, and farm stand bodies.

"Here is a motor truck of unusual strength and endurance for its capacity," the brochure proclaimed.

Yet records of what it has done show that its cost of operation is consistently low.

That is the real test of service in a commercial car. When you divide cost for fuel, tires and adjustments by the number of miles traveled and tons carried, you realize the practical economy of the Chevrolet One-Ton Truck. That is the purpose for which all Chevrolet cars are built—reliable, efficient transportation at low cost.

Speaking of cost, a General Motors internal document produced sometime later explored the cost advantages of a truck versus a horse-drawn cargo wagon and noted: "In the early days of the automobile industry, the horsemen said that while the car might compete with the carriage horse . . . it could never be hoped that it would make a serious bid for Dobbin's job between the shafts of a one- or two-horse delivery wagon."

Dobbin was the period nickname for farm and work horses, but even horsemen of that era could foresee the day, the document continued, when mechanically powered devices might be "capable of carrying five tons, 40 miles a day, or of carrying a load of passengers for 200 miles in a single day."

[It] might lessen the work of the horse by emancipating him from that kind of service, it would really help commerce because it would release so many perfectly

offered to install some bodywork from outside suppliers right on the assembly line. For example, buyers could select the standard open version or an express wagon with a canopy-style roof supported by what we would recognize today as B- and C-pillars; there was even one version with three rows of seats. Side curtains were available for use in inclement weather.

The 1920 sales brochure also showed the 490 chassis with delivery and station wagon good horses for delivery work, which, of course, would always remain the peculiar field for Dobbin.

It was pointed out that a single horse wagon making seventeen miles a day could not be touched by any motor equipment and that the two-horse wagon, traveling 20 miles a day, was perfectly secure in its job.

The conventional wisdom—and the practical experience of the later days of the horse-drawn era—was that it cost between $1.32 and $1.39 per day to keep a horse "without getting one iota of series out of him." Put that horse to work for deliveries totaling seventeen miles a day, six days a week, fifty-two weeks a year, and the cost of horse, wagon, and $2-a-day wages for the driver is $4.25 per day, or 28.3 cents per mile.

"The knell of the horse is sounded in the per mile cost of automobile delivery," the GM document reported.

It costs $2 per working day to keep a truck capable of carrying 1½ tons of freight or merchandise and costing around $2,000 in first expenditure. The driver of the car requires higher wages also, and the great companies have found that they have to pay about $3 a day for such labor. It costs just under 7 cents a mile to run such a truck and as it can make 50 miles a day without strain, the total cost of daily operation is shown to be $8.50, or 16.67 cents per mile delivered.

The report noted that, in a single day, one truck can do the work of three single-horse wagons, and suggested that there was no point in even making an argument about comparing "big" trucks with horsepower, suggesting that the big truck not only is more economical, but a horse "dragging five tons up a 6 percent grade is a cruelty that should be stopped."

According to the report, farming figured to be the last holdout for preferring horses over

At first, Chevrolet built truck chassis for customers to have "aftermarket" bodywork installed to meet their specific needs. This is one example, a 1918 Chevrolet 490 half-ton light delivery cowl chassis with what we'd now consider an open SUV body and seating.

Real Estate

Retail Phonographs

Florists

The Chevrolet Light Delivery

Retail Market

Towel Supply

Sign Hangers

And they did. For 1920, Chevrolet offered the 490 as a Light Delivery Chassis, Delivery Wagon with one seat or Delivery Wagon with three seats, and the Model T as Chassis & Cowl, Flare Board Express, or Covered Flare (sided bed).

In 1921, a new Model G was added to the mix. It was a ³/₄-ton truck, created by taking the front section of the 490 and backing it with a stronger and larger rear frame and true truck axle. The Model G Light Truck was available as a plain Chassis, Chassis & Cowl, Open Express, or Canopy Express.

The sales brochure noted:

This new Chevrolet commercial model is the product of years of experience in the design and manufacture of successful motor cars.

It is built especially to supply the demand for a three-quarter ton truck whose strength and performance equal cars of greater capacity yet whose operating expense is far less. This purpose is reflected in every detail of Model "G" construction.

While Chevrolet still didn't produce its own bodywork for its trucks, the company worked with several suppliers to help meet customer needs. For example, the GM Heritage Center holds a copy of the Commercial Automobile Bodies catalog of bodies built by the Brooklyn Commercial Body Co. of Brooklyn, New York, "especially designed to fit Chevrolet Trucks."

The catalog begins with text that still rings true today, though I've substituted the phrase "pickup truck" (in brackets) for "commercial":

A [pickup truck] body to do the work required of it, must be built with a

motor vehicles. It pointed out that "farmers bought approximately one-half of the 753,000 passenger automobiles built for the 1915 season, and there are several excellent reasons why the proportion will increase in succeeding years."

The primary reason, the report speculated, was the expansion of better roads to rural areas. As a result, it suggested, the sales of "motor trucks" also figured to grow.

complete understanding of what a [pickup truck] is called upon to do. The dependable truck must be correct in design, and be simple in construction. It must be sturdily built of durable material to withstand its loaded capacity, and be able to withstand the daily shocks and strains it must endure.

In the design and building of our trucks we have sought reliability and service at low cost. To this end we have incorporated only those mechanical principles which have proven their worth in the hardest kind of service . . .

When you buy a [pickup truck] you make an important investment.

Model 'G' Light Truck
CHASSIS WITH SEAT

Model 'G' Light Truck
CHASSIS WITH CAB

Model 'G' Light Truck
EXPRESS BODY WITH TOP

CHEVROLET

The Product of Experience

In addition to its mechanical qualities, the efficiency of a truck depends upon its convenience and ease of operation.

In this respect the Chevrolet Model "G" Light Truck affords unusual value. Careful study of general commercial needs is reflected in its complete equipment.

The open express body has been especially designed for all 'round service. Ample space is provided for all loads within its rated capacity. The four-post top may be readily removed if desired. In place, however, and equipped with side curtains, it affords protection in any weather to the merchandise transported. The upholstered seat is wide enough to accommodate three people in comfort. Controls are

conveniently located for operation with the least effort of the driver.

The electric starting motor effects a saving of fuel as well as energy. Its convenience encourages shutting off the motor even for short stops, thereby increasing the economy of operation.

Adjustable windshield, speedometer, and electric headlights adjustable for position are all standard equipment.

It is the combination of its many valuable features that makes the Chevrolet Model "G" a profitable investment. It is adaptable for a wide variety of commercial uses. It is suitable for any business in which the quick, dependable and economical transportation of merchandise is a factor.

Among the truck bodies available in the catalog are those designed for delivering furniture, a stake body for carrying heavy crates or barrels, a body fully enclosed by panels, a six-post express body with side rails and a top (but otherwise open), a cabin express with an open bed but sheltered area for the driver and a passenger, and a "combination passenger express" with sides and roof to cover multiple rows of seats but with large, unglazed window openings.

Well into the 1922 model year, Chevrolet briefly expanded its truck offerings with the addition of a fourth model, the New Superior.

For 1923, both the 490 and the Model T trucks were replaced with the half-ton Light Delivery Superior Series A (to be replaced later that model year by the updated Superior Series B). These were available as Chassis, Canopy Express, Panel, or Station Wagon. In the one-ton Utility

Express category, the Superior Series D came in Chassis, Utility Express, Cattle Body, and Delivery configurations, again with aftermarket bodywork in the various guises.

The evolution continued. In 1924, Series F (with a new front axle) replaced Series B and, a year later, this was replaced by Series K (with new rear axle and semi-elliptic springs). Meanwhile, D begat H, which now was tagged as a Utility Truck, soon succeeded by J and by M for 1925, when the truck engines were redesigned. The hundred-thousandth Chevrolet truck—a Series M one-ton—rolled off the assembly line at Janesville, Wisconsin, on June 3, 1925.

While this evolution took place, an innovative, even revolutionary, truck was progressing through the Chevrolet product pipeline and was about to appear on city streets, country lanes, and a variety of work sites around the country.

OPPOSITE: This Chevrolet brochure shows just some of the variations and uses possible with its 490 truck chassis for the 1920 model year.

ABOVE: Pages from a Chevrolet sales brochure advertising the company's new Model G light truck lineup.

A Six Sets Chevrolet Trucks Apart

Even though pickup trucks were still in their automotive infancy, Chevrolet worked throughout the 1920s and 1930s to make its trucks not only more durable but more comfortable as well.

They were also more complete as ready-to-use vehicles, serving customers' needs straight out of the showroom. Early on, buyers of a "truck" got a four-wheeled vehicle with a drivetrain, hood, cowl, front fenders, and (maybe) a set of running boards, as well as a beefed-up frame and a place for the driver to sit. But there likely was no cabin around that driver, nor what we'd recognize as a pickup truck bed behind the seat. Those were supplied by outside companies, selected by the buyer to meet specific needs and installed either by the dealership or even by the customer.

A catalog for the Brooklyn Commercial Body Co., produced late in the 1910s, shows the company's specialized truck bodies: Style 100 Furniture Body, Style 105 Stake Body, Style 113 Panel Body, Style 115 Six-Post Express, Style 119 Cabin Express body, and Style 120 Combination Passenger Express. Except for the Combination Passenger Express, all were available in the buyer's choice of green, maroon, or red. The Combination Passenger Express, with a full roof, windshield, and roll-down canvas side curtains to help protect all passengers from the elements, offered a russet brown shade of paint.

Several other companies provided truck bodywork, including Hercules, Superior, Columbia, Mifflinburg, Geneva, Springfield, Fisher Body, and Martin-Parry. This last, a company formed in 1919 when Martin Truck and Body of York, Pennsylvania, and Parry Manufacturing of Indianapolis merged, had some fifteen thousand dealer outlets across the country. It noted in its advertising the strength of the "dense long leaf southern pine . . . the supreme structural wood of the world" used in its wood-framed structures. The company also boasted in its advertising that it offered specialized commercial bodies "for farmers, contractors, express companies, produce dealers, lumber, and general draying."

For more than a decade, Martin-Parry enjoyed favored status with Chevrolet and, in 1930, the company's Indianapolis plant and commercial-body business were acquired by General Motors to produce Chevrolet truck bodies.

OPPOSITE: This 1926 Chevrolet Superior Series X is a one-ton truck that is part of the GM Heritage Center Collection. The hood fenders, lights, and powertrain were shared from Chevrolet's 1926 passenger cars. A stake bed is mounted atop the Series X chassis. *Larry Edsall*

For the 1925 model year, Chevrolet introduced a new generation of half-ton "light delivery" trucks. Known as the Superior Series K, the trucks had Fisher Body–produced cabs with "vertical ventilating" windshields, although those windshields were angled back slightly to give the trucks a more modern design. New technology included one-piece rear axles with semi-elliptic springs.

A year later, Chevrolet started producing its own complete truck bodies for its one-ton trucks, with the driver and passenger enclosed in a wood-framed, steel-covered, factory-produced cabin. For its half-ton lineup, Chevrolet added two new models for 1926: a roadster pickup—basically a Chevrolet roadster car but with a factory-installed cargo box in place of a trunk—and a "commercial roadster" with what we would recognize now as a true pickup-style truck bed.

RIGHT: Chevrolet prepared this advertisement for its dealers to sell the new Roadster Delivery pickup truck, introduced for the 1926 model year. The truck was among the first to carry truck bodywork installed right on the Chevrolet assembly line.

BELOW: This Chevrolet publicity photo shot on Detroit's Belle Isle in 1930 shows the company's Roadster Delivery pickup truck carrying four golf-club-wielding dancers from *Follow Thru*, a golf-themed musical comedy.

The strength and durability of Chevrolet trucks was dramatically demonstrated in 1927 when a Chevrolet LM series truck built in South Africa carried supplies and communications equipment from Cape Town to Stockholm, Sweden, with promotional stops in Cairo and London.

Having powered its trucks with a four-cylinder engine since the beginning, Chevrolet unveiled a revolutionary development late in 1928—one period publication called it "an epoch in motor car development"—when it introduced its new inline six-cylinder engine. While the engine—known as both the "Cast-Iron Wonder" and the "Stovebolt"—displaced only 194 cubic inches and pumped out only 46 horsepower, it provided Chevrolet with a modern powerplant well ahead of Henry Ford's launch in 1932 of his Flathead V-8.

The new engine's updated features included overhead valves and a forged and balanced crankshaft. Chevrolet saw fit to advertise that it was selling "A Six in the Price Range of the Four."

A 1928 Chevrolet Light-Delivery National AB half-ton chassis with a 35 horsepower, four-cylinder engine was priced at $495, while the 1929 International Series LD with the straight six was only 400 Depression-era dollars.

"The engine represents the latest and best in modern design and construction," Chevrolet touted in its advertising brochure. "It developed unusual power at slow engine speeds; and its dependability is beyond any question—for the five years spent in the perfection of this remarkable power plant included hundreds of thousands of miles of testing at the General Motors Proving Ground."

"The Chevrolet Six boasted ample power, excellent gas mileage, smooth operation, and

In the 1920s, Chevrolet trucks still shared their underpinnings with the company's passenger cars. Touting the strength of the chassis, this ad ran in *The Saturday Evening Post.*

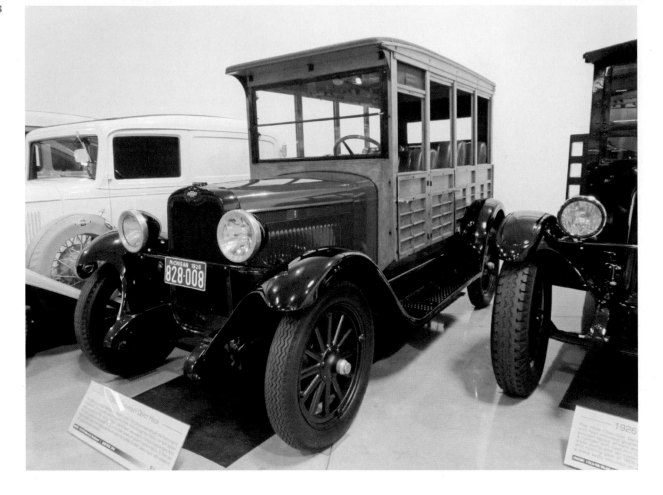

This 1928 Chevrolet Depot Hack is part of the GM Heritage Center collection. Today we recognize this body style as a "station wagon." *Larry Edsall*

unquestioned dependability, all at a low, low price," Mike Mueller writes in *Chevrolet Pickups*. "How could it get any better?"

But it did.

In 1930, Chevrolet advertising used the term "pick-up" for the first time, applying that phrase in its own specifications sheets the following year after it started producing its own all-steel truck bodies in the former Martin-Parry plant in Indianapolis. The new, all-steel cabins featured wider doors for easier entry.

The following years brought the fast progression of design improvements. The "silent synchromesh" transmission for 1932 meant no more double-clutching to shift gears. The new six-cylinder engine was enlarged and more powerful for 1933. Chevy trucks got stronger frames in 1934. Horsepower grew in 1935 and again in 1936. For 1937–38, the half-ton trucks offered a new, 85-horsepower six-cylinder engine, also featuring safety glass,

vacuum rather than hand-operated windshield wipers, reclining seats, a gas pedal instead of a button-style accelerator, and recirculating-ball steering gear.

Chevrolet also lengthened wheelbases and pickup beds, providing more room in the cabin and for carrying cargo. And the trucks started to get their own exterior styling rather than being based on passenger car design.

To showcase the advances in style, comfort, and durability, Chevrolet recruited famed racing driver and team owner Harry Hartz to do a "Safe Driving Road Test," taking a half-ton Chevrolet pickup around the perimeter of the United States.

Hartz had been a mechanic for the famous Duesenberg brothers. He was riding mechanic in the Indianapolis 500 in 1921, but in 1922 he moved into the driver's seat of a Duesenberg entry and finished second in the race. He would finish second again in 1923 and 1925.

After being badly burned in a crash in 1927, Hartz became a car owner, preparing the car that won at Indy in 1930 with Billy Arnold driving.

In the early 1930s, Hartz brought a lot of attention to DeSoto by driving one of its cars across the country backwards, with the car in reverse gear. He also set dozens of speed records at the Bonneville Salt Flats in Utah at the wheel of a Chrysler Imperial Airflow, and he set a fuel-economy record on a drive from Los Angeles to New York City.

The American Automobile Association verified the drive, even selecting a truck at random as it rolled off the assembly line at Flint, Michigan. Hartz drove a half-ton Chevy pickup through winter weather, with a 1,000-pound load in its bed, on a lap of the United States that went from Detroit to the Northwest, down the coast and across the Southern states, up the East Coast and eventually back to Detroit.

As the Chevrolet sales brochure proclaimed:

Chevrolet Truck
Breaks All Known Economy
and Dependability Records
10,244 Miles
'Round the Nation for
less than 1¢ a Mile

Through mountain passes, freezing temperatures, snow and ice; over arid deserts and mud and detours; meeting every kind of road and weather condition that the United States has to offer, a Chevrolet half-ton truck has just completed another grueling test for economy and dependability.

Chevrolet was eager to proclaim how its new six-cylinder engine not only revolutionized the light-truck marketplace, but was also being offered for the same prices as competitors' four-cylinder vehicles.

Announcing the New

CHEVROLET

The 1½ TON CHASSIS
$520

The SEDAN DELIVERY $595
The LIGHT DELIVERY CHASSIS $365
The 1½ TON CHASSIS WITH CAB $625

All prices f.o.b. factory Flint, Michigan

Ample Strength, Power and Capacity For Full 1½ Ton Loads

Outstanding among the many great assets of the new Chevrolet 6-cylinder Utility Truck is its ability to handle full 1½ ton loads without strain or overloading. Its 50-horsepower motor, 4-speed transmission, rugged rear axle and powerful brakes are more than equal to full-capacity requirements—and its over-length frame permits the use of extra-large bodies without extensions.

A SIX IN THE PRICE RANGE OF THE FOUR!

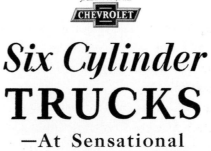

CHEVROLET

Six Cylinder TRUCKS

—At Sensational New Low Prices!

Again, Chevrolet has used the savings from its great volume production to bring to American business the greatest commercial car value in its history—

—a stronger, sturdier, more powerful line of six-cylinder trucks . . . *at sensational new low prices!*

Every factor that makes a commercial car desirable has been refined and improved in these new trucks.

The six-cylinder valve-in-head motor has been increased to 50 horsepower! The brakes have been enlarged and improved —with the front brakes of the internal-expanding type! Steering has been made easier and steadier! The rear axle is heavier and stronger! And throughout the chassis, scores of detailed improvements add to strength, durability and economy.

In addition, leading commercial body builders have designed for both the Utility and Light Delivery Chassis the finest and most complete line of bodies in Chevrolet history. No matter what your business may be—your body requirements have been anticipated.

See these new trucks at your Chevrolet dealer's—today. Check their many extra-value features. Get a trial load demonstration.

You'll find that from every standpoint—power, speed, strength, capacity, economy—here is the logical truck to own . . . the greatest commercial car value on the market today!

CHEVROLET MOTOR COMPANY, DETROIT, MICHIGAN
Division of General Motors Corporation

The brochure noted that AAA observer Stanley Reed kept daily records during the trip, showing that the truck averaged 20.74 miles per gallon and did the entire ten-thousand-plus mile drive while burning only 7½ quarts of oil, all while averaging 31 miles per hour in the pre-interstate highway era. Only one quart of water had to be added to the radiator during the drive.

"No adjustments were needed on the carburetor despite the fact that there were several consecutive days of driving in altitudes reaching from 250 feet below sea level to almost 7,000 feet above," the text noted, adding that the total cost of repairs over the course of more than ten thousand miles was a whopping 73 cents.

As daunting as Hartz' drive may have been, a larger and much more important challenge for Chevrolet, and for the nation and the world, was looming just around the corner. This time success wouldn't benefit just Chevrolet and its customers, but the population of the entire world.

CHEVY TRUCK LEGENDS: THE 1928

As part of the centennial celebration for its trucks, Chevrolet launched the Chevy Truck Legends program to recognize loyal Chevrolet truck customers. It was open to people who had driven their trucks more than 100,000 miles or who had owned multiple Chevrolet trucks during their lifetime. In this book, we're sharing some of those Legends' stories.

Greg Dunnihoo's family is only the second owner of a 1928 Chevrolet pickup truck, which he still drives in parades and enters in car shows—usually driving home with a grand champion or first-place trophy.

"The original owner used it as a delivery truck for a hardware store in Roanoke, Texas," Dunnihoo said. "This 1928 pickup is built like a rock!"

Dunnihoo's grandfather, Herbert Church Jr., and his father's brother, Weldon, bought the truck from its first owner in the early 1950s, and did a complete restoration while leaving the look original.

"They cleaned it and then put on a coat of paint, leaving scratches and dents," Dunnihoo said. "Our goal is to have it in a Chevrolet television commercial."

Volume for Victory

As it approached its thirtieth anniversary in 1941, the Chevrolet Division of General Motors was on a roll. With much of the world embroiled in war and with production restrictions in place for the final months of the year, Chevrolet was still able to produce a record of nearly 1.34 million cars and trucks. Production exceeded one hundred thousand units in nine of the months of 1941, peaking in June with 144,209 Chevrolets rolling out of assembly plants.

As early as November 1941, the US Ordnance Department contracted General Motors and Chevrolet to design and produce the first of two pilot models for an armored car by February 1, 1941. This would be a tank-like vehicle that rode on four tires instead of two tank-style metal treads.

The attack on the US Navy base at Pearl Harbor, Hawaii, on December 7 changed the focus of Chevrolet's efforts. By the end of January 1942, all but one of Chevrolet's supply or assembly plants had converted to production for the war effort. The Saginaw supply and manufacturing plant was the one exception, continuing to produce the replacement parts needed for the maintenance of the Chevrolet cars and trucks already on American roads.

"Volume for Victory" became the motto at Chevrolet facilities as they joined other Detroit automakers in what President Roosevelt termed the "Arsenal of Democracy."

Chevrolet's primary role was in the production of 4x2, 4x4, and 6x6 trucks, engines for bombers

and cargo planes, armored cars, and parts for 90mm guns and shells for various weapons, including nearly two million armor-piercing 75mm shells, as well as aluminum forging and magnesium castings for various Allied needs.

Take the 6x6 trucks as just an example. For the 4,700 required each week for the war effort, Chevrolet produced all of the sheet metal for the GMC-desgined trucks, Chevrolet and GMC produced all of the engines, Chevrolet and Timken produced all of the axles and transfer cases, and Chevrolet and GMC did all the final assembly. Chevrolet plants in Detroit, Toledo, St. Louis, and Baltimore, as well as GMC's Pontiac plant, all were involved, some working 22½ hours a day, six days a week.

The Chevrolet truck body plant in Indianapolis was responsible for producing the bearings that went into Allison, Lycoming, Pratt & Whitney, Curtiss-Wright, and Ranger aviation, diesel marine, and stationary diesel engines.

Back in 1915, when Chevrolet was a fledgling automaker, it had purchased the former

OPPOSITE: Hundreds of Chevrolet trucks await shipment to military bases around the world. Chevrolet supplied vehicles along with other equipment to the US and Allied forces during World War II.

Chevrolet-built Pratt & Whitney engines power America's mightiest warplanes, including the C-82 Flying Boxcar, shown above.

CHEVROLET

America's Automotive Leader Gears All Its Resources to

"THE BIGGEST TRANSPORT JOB OF ALL TIME"

on land ... in the air ... all around the world

BUY MORE WAR BONDS
HELP SPEED THE VICTORY

Chevrolet has produced more than 475,000 military trucks in three different types, serving our fighting men everywhere.

CHEVROLET DIVISION OF GENERAL MOTORS

Maxwell Motor Plant at Tarrytown, New York, using the facility to assemble vehicles for dealerships along the East Coast. A channel some twelve feet deep connected the plant property to the Hudson River, which provided access to export shipping lanes. During World War II, Tarrytown produced 165 4x2 military trucks each day, the vast majority of them boxed in twin-unit packs and shipped overseas. It also produced 4x2 long-wheelbase trucks and 4x4 cargo and dump trucks, again to supply the need overseas. Fisher Body, which produced bodies for many GM vehicles, also had a plant at Tarrytown; that plant was turned over to Eastern Aircraft for airplane production.

Though originally protected under the Espionage Act, 50 U.S.C., 31 and 32, here is just a partial list of Chevrolet facilities and their wartime production:

Atlanta, Georgia—Military truck assembly; wood cargo bodies for 6x6 trucks.

Bay City, Michigan—Dozens of parts for military trucks.

Buffalo, New York—Tools for machines in war-product manufacturing.

Detroit Gear & Axle—Axles for military trucks and midship propeller shafts for boats; heat-treated barrels for machine guns.

Detroit Forge—Dies for airplane propellers, bombers and fighter planes; universal joint forgings for Army trucks; landing gear strut forgings; gun mounts and guns for the Navy; forgings for bombsights and the Oerlikon gun; bearing forgings for M-4 tanks; transmission forgings for armored cars and tanks; forgings and propeller blades for patrol boats; end connections for tanks; forgings for bombers; propeller forgings and

OPPOSITE: Chevrolet also built aircraft engines that propelled a variety of military aircraft for the war effort.

ABOVE: Sometimes, aircraft powered by Chevrolet-built engines carried Chevrolet-built trucks. And sometimes, a Chevy truck carried the remains of a downed aircraft.

TREMENDOUS PRODUCTION

Meets a Tremendous Worldwide Transportation Problem

CHEVROLET TRUCKS, "thrift-carriers for the nation" in time of peace, are "victory-carriers for the nation" in time of war.

They are serving our distinguished officers and men on battlefronts all over the world with the same rugged stamina and dependability which have always characterized their performance at home.

Chevrolet has been supplying the armed forces with huge numbers of these vitally important land transports, month after month, since long before Pearl Harbor.

It has built and delivered scores of thousands of 4x4 military trucks (four-wheelers with all wheels driven)—additional thousands of 4x2's (four-wheelers with rear-wheel drive) . . . and it has made equally impressive contributions to the nation's production of 6x6 military trucks (six-wheeled vehicles with six wheels driven).

It takes tremendous production of all these units to meet America's tremendous worldwide transportation problem; and Chevrolet—largest builder of trucks in peacetime—is doing its full share to meet this need as part of its program of VOLUME FOR VICTORY.

Every Sunday Afternoon, GENERAL MOTORS SYMPHONY OF THE AIR, NBC Network

BUY WAR BONDS
SPEED THE VICTORY

CHEVROLET DIVISION OF GENERAL MOTORS

MAKING PRATT & WHITNEY ENGINES FOR B-24 LIBERATOR BOMBERS AND C-47 AND C-53 CARGO PLANES, ALUMINUM AND STEEL FORGINGS, IRON AND MAGNESIUM CASTINGS, HIGH-EXPLOSIVE AND ARMOR-PIERCING SHELLS, MILITARY TRUCKS AND MANY OTHER WAR PRODUCTS

4x2 MILITARY TRUCKS

4x4 MILITARY TRUCKS

6x6 MILITARY TRUCKS

dies for Hamilton propellers; axle forgings and other parts for US and British military trucks, heat-treated barrels for machine guns; forgings for Naval guns and tank engines; steering forgings for armored cars.

Flint, Michigan (Chevrolet assembly, pressed metal, motor plant, and Fisher Body)—Dies and castings for airplane propellers; machine work on castings for 90mm guns; 90mm guns, 75mm armor-piercing shells; tools and fixtures for tanks; engines, motors, sheetmetal and replacement parts for military trucks; tool, fixtures, and parts for sub-machine guns; M-6 armored car

ABOVE: Chevrolet trucks covered much of the globe on behalf of the US and allied military during World War II.

LEFT: In addition to 6x6 trucks, Chevrolet provided trucks to the military with six tires on two axles.

assembly; more than fifty thousand engines per year for 4x2 and 4x4 military trucks and another sixty thousand a year for 6x6 trucks.

Indianapolis, Indiana—Gun mount parts for armored cars; turret plates, tooling, and fixtures for M-3 tanks; patterns for Allison engines and Sperry bombsights; fixtures for Grumman aircraft; parts for military trucks.

Muncie, Indiana—Forgings for B-17 bombers and other airplane parts; crankcase forgings for tank engines; wing and fuselage parts; frame forgings for Scout bombers; forgings for supercharger impellers and other parts for airplane engines; dies for Allison engines; reduction gear assemblies for armored cars; aluminum forgings for bombers; forgings for landing gear struts for the B-25 bomber; transmissions and other parts for military trucks.

ABOVE: Riddled with weapon fire, a Chevrolet truck still provides a place for a soldier to rest for a few minutes.

LEFT: An ad letting America know that Chevrolet was "already on the job!" supplying the US military.

Saginaw, Michigan (Foundry and Service Manufacturing plants)—Aluminum pistons forgings for tank engines; patterns for Pratt & Whitney engines; patterns for bombs and Army canteens; aluminum piston forgings for Allison engines; tools for armored cars; transmission cases for armored cars; dies for the Hamilton propellers; motor castings, pistons and replacement parts for military trucks; tool castings for bow guns, 20mm and 75mm guns; side plates for machine guns.

St. Louis, Missouri—6x6 truck assembly.

Toledo, Ohio—Dozens of parts for military trucks.

Tonawanda, New York—Production of parts and assembly of the initial armored car prototype; production of as many as three thousand Pratt & Whitney airplane engines per month.

Meanwhile, Chevrolet's Baltimore facility became the country's largest military parts depot; the Oakland, California, assembly plant produced vehicles for military bases up and down the West Coast; and the Chevrolet Parts Department so impressed military officials that the US Army's Quartermaster Corps asked it to reorganize the massive Camp Normoyle supply center at San Antonio, Texas.

"Already On the Job!" proclaimed an advertisement that ran in several automotive publications in the spring of 1941, showing a line of Chevrolet trucks heading from the Atlanta and Oakland assembly plants to the US Army bases. The ad explained:

Months ago, in the earliest days of the emergency, there came an urgent call for trucks—*and still more trucks*—for the US

OPPOSITE TOP: Trucks and troops rolling out.

OPPOSITE LEFT: Ready for transport to foreign shores.

OPPOSITE RIGHT: Offloading overseas.

BELOW: Chevy trucks carried supplies to soldiers wherever they were fighting.

ABOVE: A Chevrolet station wagon makes its way across rugged terrain during World War II.

RIGHT: Neither mud nor snow can slow these trucks.

OPPOSITE: Gun-toting trucks are ready for battle.

FOLLOWING PAGES: A Chevrolet tanker truck refuels a row of tanks.

Army. Great numbers of Chevrolet trucks are already on the job at Army camps in all parts of the country. Thousands of additional Chevrolet trucks are on the way . . . Other thousands will continue to roll off our assembly lines as long as they are needed . . . smoothly, steadily, in ever-increasing numbers, to help meet some of the most vital needs of modern defense—*an army equipped to move swiftly over any type of ground.*

America has helped to make the Chevrolet Division of General Motors one of the largest manufacturing units in the

(Continued on page 39)

(Continued from page 34)

world; and, of course, America can count on Chevrolet to contribute its full share to the biggest job in the world—National Defense.

In the fall of 1942, another big Chevrolet ad ran in magazines from the *Saturday Evening Post, Life, Collier's,* and *Good Housekeeping* to the *Farm Journal* and *Successful Farming*:

Chevrolet—Aggressively, incomparably busy—day and night, both before and since Pearl Harbor—turning out huge quantities of many different weapons—turning out Volume Production for Victory!

Illustrating the advertisement were images of Chevrolet employees building Pratt & Whitney airplane engines, military trucks, airplane parts, and armor-piercing shells.

OPPOSITE TOP: Chevrolet trucks stationed in India.

OPPOSITE BOTTOM: A Chevrolet truck in the North African desert.

LEFT: When a makeshift airfield needed a control tower, Chevy had one ready.

BELOW: A Chevrolet truck supplying fuel.

Another ad, published in national magazines and also in publications aimed at those working the various trades—*Contractors & Engineers Monthly, Plumbing & Heating Journal, Midwestern Trucker & Shipper*—noted that Chevrolet-built military vehicles were "A Line of 'Huskies' on Hitler's Trail."

"Somewhere in Africa" these and other long lines of Chevrolet trucks are moving forward with our fighting men in irresistible pursuit of the Axis ... And all over the embattled world Chevrolet-built airplane engines, anti-aircraft guns, armor-piercing shells and other war equipment are likewise serving side by side with our fighting

RIGHT: This 1942 ad uses the "V" from the Volume for Victory slogan.

BELOW: This Chevrolet advertisement encourages those at home to buy more war bonds.

CHEVROLET

Aggressively, incomparably busy—day and night, both before and since Pearl Harbor—turning out huge quantities of many different weapons—turning out **VOLUME PRODUCTION FOR VICTORY!**

CHEVROLET — AMERICA'S FOREMOST VOLUME — DIVISION — GENERAL MOTORS
PRODUCER OF CARS AND TRUCKS — OF

Today — "All America's Working for Victory, and CHEVROLET'S DOING A LEADER'S SHARE"

America's number one job today is to step out and win this war.

That applies to all of us—to industry and agriculture—to management and labor—to every individual man and woman, regardless of whether he or she is in the armed forces or in the working forces of the nation.

All are members of the team. All have a part to play in the war effort. All have an opportunity and an obligation to serve for victory.

The Chevrolet Division of General Motors, like all other companies large and small, is proud to be a member of this all-American team and to be filling the role the government has assigned to it.

Moreover, since this organization has long enjoyed the privilege of being America's largest producer of automobiles in peacetime, it naturally has been called upon to perform tasks fully commensurate with its leadership, now that America is at war.

The Chevrolet organization is performing these tasks willingly and gladly ... performing them, not alone, but in loyal concert with the armed forces, with numerous other prime contractors and sub-contractors, with all America ... performing them on scheduled time, as you would expect a leader to do.

And just what is Chevrolet doing on behalf of America's war effort?

It is building vast numbers of Pratt & Whitney aircraft engines for the fleets of B-24 Liberator bombers and C-47 and C-53 cargo planes which are carrying the war to our Axis enemies.

It is helping to build the *armies of 90-mm.* guns which are dealing destruction to enemy tanks and planes.

It is helping to build the *multitudes of armor-piercing and high-explosive shells* which are blasting the Axis on battlefronts all over the globe.

It is helping to build the *hosts of aluminum forgings and magnesium castings* which are needed by every aircraft producer in America.

It is helping to build the *columns of military trucks* which are serving our fighting men in every part of the world.

All in all, it is helping to build millions upon millions of units, not only for its own projects, but also for 123 other war producers, just as others, in turn, are serving and supplying Chevrolet.

It has not been easy to take this huge organization, with its highly skilled engineering and manufacturing personnel—its far-flung factories and assembly plants—its intricate machinery and equipment—and convert it, almost overnight, from peacetime to war production.

Any more than it is easy to plan the grand strategy of war or to lead an army into battle.

But the main point is that the job has been done—as all jobs can always be done by Americans working together—and there will be no lag and no let-up for the duration.

Today, all America's working for victory. ... And today, too, Chevrolet is doing a leader's share.

CHEVROLET DIVISION OF **GENERAL MOTORS**

★ ★ ★ **BUY MORE WAR BONDS ··· SPEED THE VICTORY** ★ ★ ★

men . . . they're the world's best fighting men, and they deserve the world's best equipment—in a great, growing, inexhaustible stream—in Volume for Victory!

While production of vehicles for civilian use was halted in late January 1940, Chevrolet was allowed to resume limited production of trucks for vital domestic uses early in 1944, primarily for farming and firefighting. Not until the early fall of 1945 did vehicles for American consumers arrive from Chevrolet assembly plants.

ABOVE: It takes two teams to win a war, according to this advertisement: one on the battlefields and another back home.

RIGHT: The bowtie emblem in military service.

Trucks for the Postwar Building Boom

Even during the war, 56,000 civilian-style Chevrolet pickup trucks were produced to meet the needs of the country's service industries, tradesmen, and manufacturing plants. Those trucks were based on prewar designs. After the end of the war, work began on a new vehicle for the postwar recovery, a truck that could meet the pent-up demand for new pickups while also serving as an important tool for the housing and commercial building boom about to sweep the country as soldiers, sailors, and other military personnel returned home.

Preliminary work on a new pickup design had begun as early as 1942, with clay models showing headlights integrated into front fenders and a tall hood a year later. Late in 1939, General Motors established a separate truck design studio led by Luther "Lu" Stier, who had been working on Chevrolet passenger car design.

"Advance-Design" was the theme for this new generation of Chevrolet trucks, their development led by chief engineer John G. Wood. The unveiling included ninety-nine models built over nine wheelbases, covering everything from pickups to panels to platforms, from carryall suburbans to platform and stakes trucks, and from chassis with cabs to those without—but ready for special bodywork, including school bus bodies, to be bolted atop their frames.

"There is a Chevrolet Truck to Fit Your Business" proclaimed a foldout mailer brochure sent to potential customers. Below those words were colorful illustrations of the various models—1500 Series, 2100 Series, 3600 Series, 3800 Series, 4000 Series, 5000 and 6000 Series—including the gross vehicle weight options available within each series.

The Chevy trucks that went into production in May 1947 were presented as "the trucks of a thousand uses"—again, designed to meet needs that customers may not yet have realized they had—and featuring more room for cargo, with "built-in power," "built-in stamina," and "built-in safety."

"This time truck buyers knew full well that they were looking at the future, not living in the past," Mike Mueller writes of the new postwar Chevrolet trucks in *Chevrolet Pickups*.

ABOVE: A cowgirl lassoes her new 1947 Chevrolet Loadmaster Heavy Duty Cab Chassis.

RIGHT: In the styling studio, a full-scale clay model of the 1947 Chevrolet Loadmaster Cab-over-Engine.

Overall impressions were newer than new, thanks first and foremost to Chevrolet's sensational "Load Proportioned" restyle that owed nothing to car-line trends or pre-war fads. Modernized lines were more pleasing as fender tops, hoodline, and cab roof seemed to work together aesthetically far more cooperatively than ever before.

As the war ended, Mueller notes, Chevrolet had surveyed truck owners across the country about their needs and identified one major complaint: cabs were too small and uncomfortable, especially if you needed to wedge three people inside. Another issue was safety,

especially from the aspect of the driver's limited visibility from inside the pickup cab.

The Advance-Design trucks featured doors that were four inches wider, making cab access much easier. Glass area increased by 15 percent, and now there was an option to add two small curved windows to the rear corners of the cab. The cab and seat were also widened and the seat redesigned so that the driver's view was optimized whether the seat was moved fore or aft. The new seat also offered a reclining back.

According to the Society of Automotive Historians (SAH), the new Chevy trucks were "unlike anything built to that time."

"Round and juicy" was the description offered by Chuck Jordan, who joined the GM Design staff in 1949 and spent time in Stier's truck studio. He would play a major role in the future of pickup truck design, becoming head of all GM Design from 1986 to 1992.

"Their overall shape and detailing were thoroughly modern at the time," according to

Can you find all the new Chevrolet trucks?

Light Loads or Heavy . . . Good Roads or Bad
IT'S A CHEVROLET JOB!

Loaded with power, Chevrolet trucks with the great Loadmaster 105-h.p. engine have what it takes for rough ground and the long, hard pulls. Certified ratings prove that these Chevrolet trucks provide *more net horse-power*—power delivered at the clutch—than any of the five other leading standard equipped conventional trucks in this weight class, 13,000 to 16,000 lbs. G.V.W.* With this extra get-up-and-go, Chevrolet trucks serve you better . . . and cut your costs, too.

You save time on the road, money on operations, and—with Chevrolet's built-for-the-load construction—spend less on maintenance. That all adds up to low cost per ton mile—on every mile of *every* job! It's one of the many reasons why Chevrolet trucks are the nation's biggest truck values, and the choice of more truck operators than any other make. But get the rest of the reasons for Chevrolet truck popularity before you buy any truck. See your Chevrolet dealer.

Gross Vehicle Weight.

CHEVROLET

ADVANCE-DESIGN TRUCKS

CHEVROLET MOTOR DIVISION, GENERAL MOTORS CORPORATION
DETROIT 2, MICHIGAN

If it takes more power . . . and top payloads
IT'S A CHEVROLET JOB!

Big job? That's one for Chevrolet trucks with Loadmaster 105-h.p. engine. They're loaded with power—*greater net horse-power than any of the five most popular standard equipped makes in their weight class*, 13,000 to 16,000 lbs. G.V.W.* And here's the payoff on payloads, too. Chevrolet's economy of operation and upkeep, and rock-solid construction let you deliver the goods at *low cost per ton mile*. But that isn't all! In every other way, Chevrolet is a leader. When you see these trucks you'll know it for fact. You'll know why they outsell every other make, year after year! See your Chevrolet dealer.

Gross Vehicle Weight.

CHEVROLET

ADVANCE-DESIGN TRUCKS

CHEVROLET MOTOR DIVISION, GENERAL MOTORS CORPORATION
DETROIT 2, MICHIGAN

ABOVE LEFT: A national magazine ad in the fall of 1950 showcases the capabilities of Chevrolet's newest trucks.

ABOVE RIGHT: Chevrolet trucks were ready for the postwar building boom.

RIGHT: Chevrolet's postwar Advance-Design truck line included a vehicle to meet every possible need a customer might have.

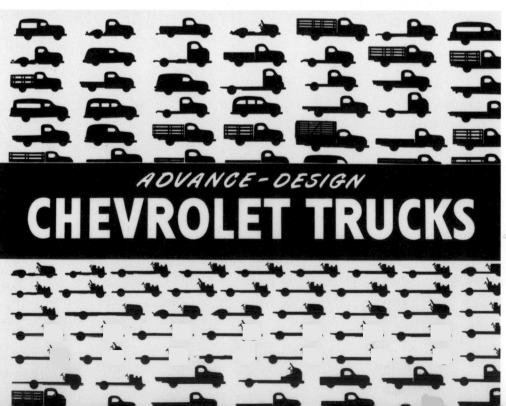

LEFT: Scale models show the possible details as the final Advance-Design truck styling is selected.

BELOW: Close-up of the postwar grille.

the SAH historians. "They looked surprisingly simple, yet these trucks had a rugged elegance that was wholly without precedent."

The Chevy sales brochure notes that:

Increased load capacity is provided in the new Chevrolet pick-up trucks by the elimination of wheelhouses. Front panels, tail-gate and platform are strong and more durable. Wide running boards, available on model 3104 at extra cost, allow the operator to stand closer to the body for loading and delivery.

Not only was the entire front structure of the truck strengthened, but the floor was designed and engineered to relieve panel stress, with welded-type curls on the front end panel and

CHEVROLET *Advance Design* TRUCKS
NEW

see the cab that "breathes"

SEE YOUR LOCAL CHEVROLET DEALER

end-gate adding rigidity. The pickup bed itself was 50 inches wide, had stake pockets within the side braces, and a wood floor with flush skid strips designed to prevent mud from working its way underneath.

Like other new Chevy trucks, the 1500 Series (also known as the EP Series) was equipped with "the cab that 'breathes.'"

"Chevrolet's Greatest Contribution to Driver Comfort . . . with 30 Advance-Design Features for Comfort, Convenience and Safety!" the brochure proclaimed of the "larger, roomier, safer" passenger compartment in its "Advance-Design" trucks. The brochure included the entire list of thirty items, from 1-All-steel, completely welded, without an open joint or seam to 30-Battery within easy reach for servicing.

OPPOSITE TOP: The "cab that breathes" was another selling point for Chevrolet's postwar trucks, which offered new cabin ventilation systems.

OPPOSITE BOTTOM: Advance-Design pickup in its final clay before production.

ABOVE: A truck cab works its way through the assembly plant.

LEFT: Trucks undergo final inspection before being shipped to dealers.

FOR MAXIMUM ALLOWABLE LOADS ON ANY ROAD

CHEVROLET *Advance-Design* TRUCKS

RIGHT: Chevrolet had a truck to carry seemingly any possible load.

BELOW: A look at the chassis beneath Chevrolet's trucks.

ADVANCE-DESIGN CHEVROLET TRUCKS

VALVE-IN-HEAD ENGINES • DIAPHRAGM SPRING CLUTCH • SYNCHRO-MESH TRANSMISSIONS • HYPOID REAR AXLES • DOUBLE-ARTICULATED BRAKES • WIDE-BASE WHEELS • ADVANCE-DESIGN STYLING • BALL-TYPE STEERING • UNIT-DESIGN BODIES

Here's what's underneath Advance-Design value

It's what you'll find *beneath* the body of a Chevrolet truck that tells you what you want to know. For here is centered Chevrolet's world-famous power, added strength and rugged durability. These are the things that bring you *more miles of low-cost performance . . . more years of profitable service*. See these trucks—from the bottom up and from the top down—before you decide. You're sure to find the one that best fits your needs among the 81 models on 9 wheelbases. Check the great Valve-in-Head engine, Synchro-Mesh transmission, Hypoid rear axle—plus the many other features that tell you Chevrolet trucks are built to do your job best! See your Chevrolet dealer today.

CHEVROLET MOTOR DIVISION, *General Motors Corporation*, DETROIT 2, MICHIGAN

PREFERRED BY MORE USERS

THAN THE NEXT TWO MAKES COMBINED!

In between were such features as an optional new ventilation system (inhaling fresh air and exhaling used air for year-round comfort), better visibility ("observation-car vision," the brochure notes), "Nu-Vue" rear-corner windows, improved weather sealing, concealed hinges, two bottom-mounted windshield wipers providing larger sweep coverage on a windshield that was 22 percent larger than on previous trucks, larger defroster openings, redesigned instrument panel (with instruments grouped for driver convenience), a 30-amp fuse box, and even provision for a push-button radio, cigar lighter, and ashtray.

In a further nod to the pickup's working status, a tool compartment measuring 50 x 19½ x 6 inches was located beneath the seat.

The cabin, now mounted on rubber-cushioned insulators, provided for a seat that was 3¾ inches wider, and offered 8 inches more hip room and 3½ inches more space across the shoulders. There also was more leg room, and the seat back could be reclined with "finger-tip ease." Seat cushions featured five rows of coil springs for comfort.

Chevrolet referred to the new cabin's "Battleship" construction, which increased strength and durability. *The Standard Catalog of Chevrolet Trucks* refers to the new cab as featuring "Unisteel" styling.

The trucks' redesigned lines are also characterized as "neat and uncluttered." One factor was the change in door hinges, from exposed hinges used on prewar trucks to new hinges hidden within the truck cab's sheet metal.

According to the *Standard Catalog*:

The grilles had five broad horizontal bars topped by a broad hood ornament containing a blue bow tie and vermilion Chevrolet lettering. Rectangular parking lights were placed in chrome housings at the ends of the uppermost pair of grille bars. A painted grille was standard equipment and a two-piece, flat windshield was used.

Front and rear fenders retained their individual forms. Their rounded shape, in conjunction with the rounded corners of the body, gave the Chevrolet trucks a more up-to-date appearance.

The *Standard Catalog* also notes that the Chevrolet commercial body plant in Indianapolis doubled its production and that new truck assembly plants opened in Cleveland, Los Angeles, and Flint to build the new Advance-Design vehicles.

Powering the new pickups was Chevrolet's Thriftmaster Six, an inline, overhead-valve, six-cylinder engine

ABOVE RIGHT: Advance-Design pickup trucks were a hit with those involved in postwar building—and with farmers who fed all those returning service personnel.

RIGHT: This ad emphasizes the status gained from making deliveries in a new Chevrolet truck.

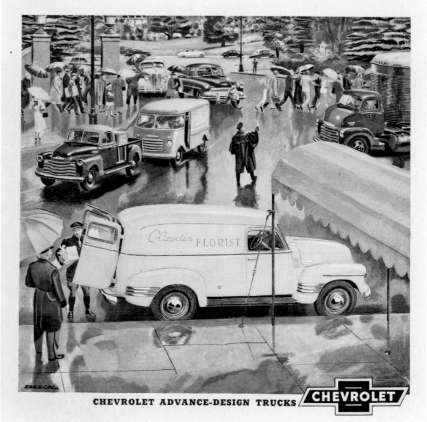

Add **prestige** to your deliveries with **CHEVROLET TRUCKS!**

Whatever you haul or deliver, a Chevrolet Advance-Design Truck tells a lot about your business.

It looks successful, modern, efficient. It's a travelling advertisement that makes a favorable impression everywhere it goes.

What's more, a Chevrolet Truck reflects your good judgment. It's engineered and built to do your particular job . . . and do it at rock-bottom cost of operation and upkeep. Its list price is less than any truck of

comparable specifications . . . and it brings the highest resale value, traditionally, of any truck in the low-price field.

Let Chevrolet Advance-Design Trucks, with their great Valve-in-Head Thriftmaster or Loadmaster engines, take over on your truck assignments. They look like good business because they *are* good business . . . and your Chevrolet dealer can show you why. See him now. Chevrolet Motor Division, General Motors Corporation, Detroit 2, Michigan.

(Continuation of equipment and trim illustrated is dependent on availability of material)

CHEVROLET ADVANCE-DESIGN TRUCKS **CHEVROLET**

with "Blue-flame" combustion displacing 216.5 cubic inches and pumping out 90 horsepower and 174 pound-feet of torque. That power reached the rear axle through a three-speed transmission with a floor-mounted shifter.

Chevy claimed its truck engines did "more work on a gallon [of] gasoline" than those from any of its competitors.

For the 1948 model year, Chevy truck buyers were offered a new four-speed synchromesh transmission that eliminated the need for double-clutching.

The 1500 and 3100 (½-ton) sedan delivery and pickup, respectively, rode on

ABOVE: At a local fair, a Chevrolet dealer advertises Advance-Design pickup trucks.

LEFT: Farm magazines ran this advertisement across the country in the spring of 1951.

OPPOSITE TOP: Night deliveries at the port are featured in the dramatic artwork for this Chevrolet truck ad. Note the variety of trucks included in a single advertisement.

OPPOSITE BOTTOM: Chevrolet truck advertisement from the spring of 1953.

Around the clock, across the nation—more Chevrolet trucks in use than any other make

Busy trade and bustling traffic call for these 1953 Chevrolet truck advantages . . .

One of the toughest jobs any truck can tackle is moving America's goods from terminal to market. Tight loading schedules call for complete dependability. Ease of handling is a must. Stamina, power and economy are needed to make deliveries within close limits of time and cost.

And those are the very reasons why Chevrolet trucks have long been first choice of truckers across the nation!

Now, in 1953, Chevrolet trucks are even better equipped to handle any job. For these are the ruggedest Chevrolet trucks ever built—with stronger, sturdier construction in all models to bring you new dependability, new stamina and even lower over-all costs.

You'll find, too, solid superiority in performance and handling ease. You'll find exceptional efficiency and economy that have made Chevrolet trucks famous throughout the world.

Yet with all their outstanding advantages, model for model, these great 1953 Chevrolet trucks list for less than any other trucks with comparable capacity and specifications.

For the right truck for your job, see your Chevrolet dealer. Chevrolet Division of General Motors, Detroit 2, Michigan.

Engineers' reasons why Chevrolet trucks work for less around the clock

More pulling power. Advanced Loadmaster engine brings you a new higher compression ratio of 7.1 to 1 and even greater horsepower than before. This greatly improved engine is optional on 4000 Series heavy-duty trucks, standard on 5000 and 6000 heavy-duty Series and Forward-Control models. On light- and medium-duty models, Chevrolet's great Thriftmaster engine provides all the power you need with outstanding economy.

More stopping power. Big, powerful "Torque-Action" brakes both front and rear on all models, up to 4000 Series heavy-duty trucks make

greater stopping power. Heavy-duty trucks in 4000, 5000 and 6000 heavy-duty Series use extra-large "Torque-Action" brakes in front, "Twin-Action" type in rear. Both provide greater stopping power, greater durability.

More staying power. Heavier, stronger, more durable construction means greater ruggedness and stamina for all 1953 Chevrolet trucks. Long famous for handling the roughest jobs day in and day out, Chevrolet trucks are now brawnier, sturdier than ever.

More economy. The new and greater stamina of 1953 Chevrolet

trucks, plus extra gasoline economy in heavy-duty models with improved Loadmaster engine reduces hauling costs per ton-mile, brings you greater over-all economy throughout long years of service.

Easier Ball-Gear steering. Steering power is transmitted through free-rolling balls eliminating friction of metal sliding on metal. Steering effort is materially reduced, wear on moving parts is less.

Smoother shifting. Synchro-Mesh transmission provides quick, quiet safe shifting, eliminates need for double-clutching and is extra-rugged for extra-long life.

SEE THE DINAH SHORE SHOW ON TV—Every Tues. and Thurs. Evenings. NBC-TV Network

 CHEVROLET

There's a thrifty Chevrolet truck for every kind of job

Tall timber or a city's bustling streets—more Chevrolet trucks in use than any other make

How Chevrolet trucks are engineered and powered to handle heavy loads over rough roads . . .

The crushing weight of mammoth logs rests the stamina and power of any truck. It is final proof of qualities carefully "engineered in." And a truck that handles such tremendous loads yet retains efficiency and easy handling characteristics is a truck to depend on for *any* kind of job.

Chevrolet for 1953 is such a truck. Typical of its fine engineering is the splined rear axle to hub connection on heavy-duty

models. Driving splines mate directly with wheel hubs to distribute stress evenly, eliminate loose axle shaft bolts and grease leaks. This is just one example of how every Chevrolet truck is factory-matched to the job. And in 1953 Chevrolet has even greater heavy-duty power than before.

Already thousands of satisfied users have discovered Chevrolet trucks are engineered for new dependability, new

ruggedness and for even greater over-all economy in 1953.

Best of all, they list for less than any other trucks of comparable capacity and specifications.

Let your Chevrolet dealer show you how much more you get with Chevrolet trucks—and how much less you need pay! Chevrolet Division of General Motors, Detroit 2, Michigan.

Advantages "engineered in" to keep Chevrolet trucks working longer for less

More pulling power. Advanced Loadmaster engine brings you a new higher compression ratio of 7.1 to 1 and even greater horsepower than before. This greatly improved engine is optional on 4000 Series heavy-duty trucks, standard on 5000 and 6000 heavy-duty Series and Forward-Control models. On light- and medium-duty models, Chevrolet's great Thriftmaster engine provides all the power you need with outstanding economy.

More stopping power. Big, powerful "Torque-Action" brakes both front and rear on all models up to 4000 Series heavy-duty trucks make full use of truck momentum for

greater stopping power. Heavy-duty trucks in 4000, 5000 and 6000 heavy-duty Series use extra-large "Torque-Action" brakes in front, "Twin-Action" type in rear. Both provide greater stopping power, greater durability.

More staying power. Heavier, stronger, more durable construction means greater ruggedness and stamina for all 1953 Chevrolet trucks. Long famous for handling the roughest jobs day in and day out, Chevrolet trucks are now brawnier, sturdier than ever.

More economy. The new and greater stamina of 1953 Chevrolet

trucks, plus extra gasoline economy in heavy-duty models with improved Loadmaster engine reduces hauling costs per ton-mile, brings you greater over-all economy throughout long years of service.

Easier Ball-Gear steering. Steering power is transmitted through free-rolling balls eliminating friction of metal sliding on metal. Steering effort is materially reduced, wear on moving parts is less.

Smoother shifting. Synchro-Mesh transmission provides quick, quiet safe shifting, eliminates need for double-clutching and is extra-rugged for extra-long life.

(Continuation of standard equipment and trim illustrated is dependent on availability of material)

 **CHEVROLET**

TUNE IN THE DINAH SHORE SHOW ON NBC
Television: Every Tues. and Thurs. Evenings—Radio: Every Mon. and Fri. Evenings

There's a thrifty Chevrolet truck for every kind of job

It's better business to buy Chevrolet Trucks

New, bigger load space saves time and extra trips!

New 1954 Chevrolet trucks save you time on the job in *two* important ways with new, roomier Advance-Design bodies.

First of all, they let you haul bigger, bulkier loads. The new pickup bodies are deeper . . . the new stake and platform bodies are wider and longer. There's bigger space for cargo so that you can move more of it in fewer trips. You not only save time, but you save on operating costs as well!

In addition, these great new Chevrolet trucks for 1954 make loading and unloading faster and easier than ever before. You'll find that floor-to-ground heights are lower in pickup, stake and platform bodies. As a result, there's less lifting to do—and less lifting means time saved at both ends of your trips.

New Chevrolet truck bodies bring you other big new advantages, too. Pickup bodies, for example, have a tailgate that seals tight when closed to prevent leakage of grain, sand, gravel and other loose loads. Stake and platform bodies feature a stronger rub rail for increased protection, and rounded rear corners to help prevent damage when maneuvering in close quarters and backing up to loading docks.

Another thing you'll like about these new bodies is their extra ruggedness. They're built to stand up under tough jobs and keep coming back for more!

Plan now to see your Chevrolet dealer and find out about *all* the money-saving new features offered by America's lowest-priced truck line. . . . Chevrolet Division of General Motors, Detroit 2, Michigan.

CHEVROLET ADVANCE-DESIGN TRUCKS

Completely new '54 Chevrolet trucks offer all these brand-new features—

NEW AUTOMATIC TRANSMISSION:* Great new driving ease! Truck Hydra-Matic is offered not only on ½- and ¾-ton, but on 1-ton models, too!

NEW ENGINE POWER AND FUEL ECONOMY: Bigger, brawnier

"Thriftmaster 235" engine. Rugged, durable "Loadmaster 235" engine. All-new "Jobmaster 261" engine.*

NEW COMFORTMASTER CAB: Offers new comfort and safety. New one-piece curved windshield gives extra visibility.

NEW RIDE CONTROL SEAT*: Seat cushion and back move as a unit to "float" you over bumps. Eliminates annoying back-rubbing.

NEW CHASSIS RUGGEDNESS: You get extra strength and stamina! Heavier axle shafts in two-ton models . . . bigger, more durable clutches and more rigid frames in *all* models.

NEW ADVANCE-DESIGN STYLING: New, massive front-end design. New parking lights show the full width of the truck.

*Optional at extra cost. Ride Control Seat is available on all cab models. "Jobmaster 261" engine on 2-ton models.

MORE CHEVROLET TRUCKS IN USE THAN ANY OTHER MAKE! CHEVROLET

116-inch wheelbases, while the 3600 (¾-ton) provided 125.25 inches between front and rear axle centers. The 3600 trucks also got a new full-floating hypoid rear axle designed to enhance load-carrying capacity.

A significant change in the Advance-Design trucks, done to enhance safety, involved repositioning the fuel tank to the right-side frame rail between the cab and the rear axle.

Mueller notes that the Advance-Design design remained in production until the middle of the 1955 model year, "with no complaints from customers who continued to make Chevrolet number one year in, year out."

While the basic truck remained in production, there were upgrades and updates, including the four-speed transmission in 1948. The following year, 3100, 3600, or 3800 trim badges appeared, with the gear-shift lever moved to the steering column; a revised Thriftmaster six-cylinder engine featured a "Power Jet" downdraft carburetor and larger exhaust valves, good for two more horsepower, and even better seat padding came for 1950. Brakes were improved and door vent windows were added for 1951, though Korean conflict war restrictions greatly reduced the use of chromed brightwork. Push-button door handles with an optional lock on the driver's door arrived for 1952,

OPPOSITE: Full-size drawings hung in the Chevrolet design studio for stylists and executives to consider various front-end treatments for the 1954 model year.

CONVENTIONAL GROUP-2
Chevrolet Cab

CAB WIDTH INSIDE 59

Postwar Advance-Design Chevrolet trucks were also shown with updated styling, including a futuristic design for a new-car carrier.

as did a foot-operated parking brake. Then, for 1953, tinted glass and an optional side-mounted spare tire became available.

Even though an entirely new generation of Chevrolet pickups was introduced mid-year in 1955, there were many changes to the Advance-Design vehicles for 1954, including a one-piece curved windshield, new grille design with the word "Chevrolet" stamped into the header bar and painted in Waldorf White, new instrument panel with recessed gauges and with defroster openings the full width of the windshield, and a new steering wheel to provide a clearer view of the new gauge clusters.

The truck frame was strengthened and the bed floor lowered by two inches for loading and enhanced cargo capacity. But perhaps the biggest news was the availability of an optional Hydra-matic automatic transmission and the use of the larger, higher-compression, 112-horsepower Thriftmaster 235 six-cylinder as the standard engine.

Chevrolet would roll out not only an all-new pickup truck for the 1955 model year, but one offering both a V-8 engine and the most modern design ever seen to that time on an American pickup. But the road to those new trucks had been paved by the Advance-Design pickups, which were the sales leaders every year they were in production.

CHEVY TRUCK LEGENDS: ONE TRUCK, FIVE GENERATIONS

Tom Kallenberg's daily driver is a 2016 Chevrolet Silverado. But he says his "real" Chevy truck is the one his grandfather bought new from Browder Chevrolet in Union City, Tennessee. The truck is a 1954 Chevrolet 3100 "five window."

"I was seven years old and clearly remember the day my pa drove it home," Kallenberg said. "It's been in the family for sixty-two years now."

Kallenberg learned to drive in the truck when he was around eleven years old and had to help load hay.

"I did some restoration," he said, not unexpected for a truck of a certain age, "but the engine and all running gear are original and stock.

"My kids drove it to high school. My grandson just got his driver's license and will be the fifth generation of our family to drive it."

The Kallenberg's 1954 Chevrolet 3100 has been driven over 200,000 miles through the generations.

"It's never been out of the family," he added. "It's a treasure!"

Task-Force Style

America was on the move, hurrying toward the horizon as it sped through the midpoint of the 1950s. Disneyland opened in California, and the Mickey Mouse Club made its television debut. Racial segregation in schools was declared unconstitutional. Jonas Salk's vaccine for polio was approved. The St. Lawrence Seaway opened the Great Lakes to oceangoing ships. The National Interstate and Defense Highways Act was about to be introduced in Congress.

Automakers were hustling to meet the country's transportation needs. At Chevrolet, the 1955 model year produced a nearly complete makeover of all of its vehicles, cars and trucks; "nearly complete," because, while the Corvette got a new V-8 engine, it retained its original styling. All other cars were redesigned, looking more fit and trim—all the better, as Dinah Shore encouraged everyone within earshot to "see the USA in a Chevrolet."

Should you choose, you could see the landscape fly by in whatever Chevy you drove, since that new Chevrolet V-8 engine was available not only in the Corvette, but in sedans, coupes, convertibles, and even in a new two-door station wagon called the Nomad.

With so many changes to the Chevrolet passenger car lineup, the 1955 American automotive model year launched with what were basically Chevrolet pickup and other trucks carried over with only minor updating from 1954. The wait for something truly new was paid off—and dramatically so—in late

March 1955, when Chevrolet launched its new Task-Force truck series.

Featuring seventy-five new models constructed atop fifteen wheelbase dimensions, the 1955 Chevrolet trucks were designed to take on a variety of tasks. With the availability of that new V-8 engine, as well as the tried-and-true inline six-cylinder powerplants, these new trucks promised to have the force to carry out whatever task they were assigned.

"Completely new cab, single-unit bodies and sheetmetal structures combine an ultra-modern appearance with many advantages in driver convenience and comfort," Chevrolet said in a news release when the trucks launched. "All series are affected by extensive dimensional changes which are reflected in reduced overall height, greater utility and increased stability. Conventional models have shorter wheelbases for greater maneuverability and better weight distribution."

OPPOSITE: Just as this marketing illustration suggests, the beautiful Chevrolet Cameo Carrier demonstrates that it's still a tough truck as it takes on a rough, bricked section of the General Motors Proving Ground test track in Milford, Michigan.

Modern Design for Modern Hauling
ALL-NEW CHEVROLET *Task-Force* PICK-UP TRUCKS

ABOVE: Task-Force was the name of Chevrolet's new-generation of trucks launched for the 1955 model year. Even without the Cameo Carrier, the trucks were stylish, with a forward-leaning, "load-pulling" look designed to add some style to the worksite.

OPPOSITE BOTH: Regardless of their size, Chevrolet's Task-Force trucks looked right at home with the mid-century modern design of the mid-1950s.

FOLLOWING PAGES: With its smooth lines and large wheel covers, the Chevrolet Cameo Carrier brought revolutionary styling and sophistication to the pickup truck market.

Equip a truck with Chevy's new 265-cubic-inch V-8 engine and "load-pulling" was much more than a design theme.

To help pull whatever load, the trucks were built on new frames with parallel side-member construction. Front suspension was improved with longer I-beams, longer and wider but softer front springs (for a smoother ride), and wider tires. Rear springs were optimized for enhanced ride quality. Steering geometry was improved, with power steering available on most models; ditto power brakes. Six-cylinder engines were improved with more efficient (and quieter) cooling and lubrication systems. The three-speed transmission was strengthened. Higher-capacity rear axles were used.

Chevy trucks were the first to get wraparound, "Sweep-Sight" windshields like those just introduced on the stunning LeSabre concept car, and an optional wraparound rear window was offered as well. The dramatic visual difference involved new and advanced exterior styling, with forward-slanting body and sheetmetal lines providing a capable, "load-pulling" appearance that was enhanced by hooded headlamps, an egg-crate grille design, and a straight-through styling from the front fenders to the rear boundary of the cab side. The overall effect of the Task-Force design brought style to the work site.

Pushing that theme from the jet age into the space age was a limited-production version of the new pickup, the Cameo Carrier. Officially designated as Model 3124, the Cameo Carrier looked unlike any truck ever seen on an American roadway. It was part pickup and part Corvette!

Just like the Corvette, the Cameo Carrier could be equipped with Chevrolet's new V-8 engine, and it also got fiberglass rear body

(Continued on page 65)

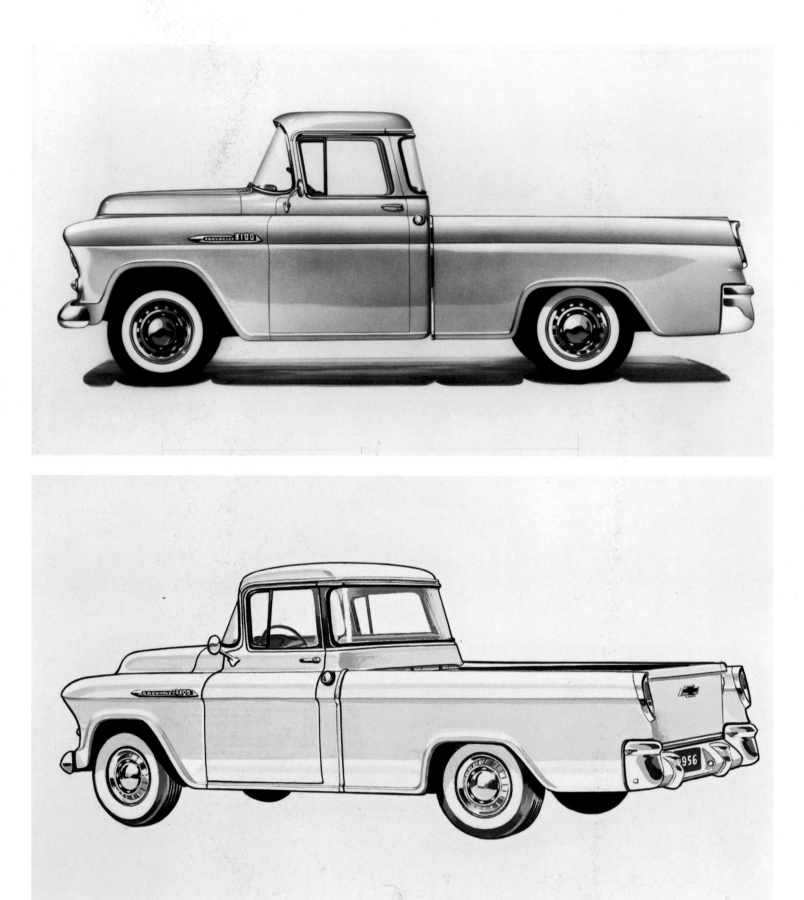

(Continued from page 61)

panels from the Moulded Fiberglass Company of Ashtabula, Ohio, the same supplier of the Corvette's composite bodywork.

The new composite bodysides transformed the truck's appearance, covering the rear wheelwell bulges with a smooth panel, accented by a character line that extended the full length of the truck just below the shoulder. These trucks also got fiberglass panels that hid the tailgate hinges, new tail lamps, and a hidden rear compartment that housed the spare tire.

Chevrolet noted that this new and "most glamorous" of truck designs was "styled for the personal transportation of many types of people—ranchers, farmers, suburbanites and outdoor sports people." The styling promised to attract attention, favorable impressions, and prestige for a business, combining glamour with utility and beauty with practicality. But

ALL: Chevrolet's Task-Force trucks came in a variety of sizes, each designed to fit a particular customer's needs and specific task requirements. For particular customers, it was important to look good at work, which explained the appeal of the Cameo Carrier with its unique styling cues.

A full-scale clay model of the 1955 Cameo Carrier displayed in the Chevrolet design department.

the truck also remained practical: the Cameo Carrier had the same load-carrying capacity as the standard Model 3100 Chevy pickup.

The Cameo Carrier's design was penned by Chuck Jordan, who grew up helping in his grandparents' orange groves in Southern California, where Jordan learned to drive his grandfather's big 12-speed Moreland truck and became fascinated with large work vehicles.

Jordan wanted to be a car designer. He thought it would be advantageous to understand the mechanical aspects of such vehicles. He studied mechanical engineering at the Massachusetts Institute of Technology (MIT), but didn't neglect his design education,

returning home each summer to attend the Chouinard Institute of Art in Los Angeles.

At age 19, Jordan won the national first prize in the General Motors Fisher Body Craftsman Guild's model-building contest and got to spend four days at the GM design studios in Detroit, where he was essentially promised a job after his graduation in 1948. Because of his interest in trucks (the title of his graduate thesis at MIT was "Heavy-Duty Mack Truck Styling"), he was assigned to Lu Stier's truck studio, where he led design for the production version of the Cameo Carrier.

Jordan left GM to serve in the air force during the Korean conflict, but kept sketching

LEFT: Cameo Carriers were available in a variety of two-tone paint combinations.

BELOW: The 1955 version of the Cameo Carrier undergoes the final phases of Its prepruduction testing.

ABOVE: New Task-Force trucks for 1955—a Cameo Carrier (left) and the "Suburban" version of the 3100 Series truck—undergo high-speed testing on the big oval track at the GM Proving Grounds.

trucks while stationed in Florida. When he returned to GM, he designed an articulated crawler tractor (for a GM heavy-equipment division) and a streamlined train (GM also was involved in railroading). Bill Mitchell, the No. 2 person in the GM Design, suggested the young designer/engineer focus on a career in cars. This was good advice: Jordan went on to design the Buick Centurion concept car, become chief of the Cadillac studio, lead styling at GM's Opel division in Germany, and ultimately become only the fourth person to oversee all of GM Design.

First, though, he worked in Stier's truck studio. His responsibilities there included developing the overall look of Task-Force trucks. According to Mike Mueller in *Chevy Trucks*, Jordan's Cameo Carrier was a revolutionary benchmark in pickup design, proving,

that trucks could look damn near as pretty as their automotive cousins and still be tough . . . It was the 1955 Chevy trucks' newfound style and flair—punctuated most dramatically by the cool, clean Cameo with its tantalizing fiberglass tail—that helped turn the corner sharper than ever before toward trucks' rampant popularity today.

Chevrolet model 10203 in foreground. At left, Cameo Carrier model 3124.

When schedules are tight... shine! New Task·Force 57

these trucks really Chevrolet Trucks

The "Big Wheel" in trucks

You can count on Chevrolet trucks to stay on schedule right around the clock. That's why you see them so many places where the job just won't wait for a truck that's late!

PROVED ON THE ALCAN HIGHWAY ... CHAMPS OF EVERY WEIGHT CLASS!

When *aren't* schedules tight these days? That's why you need a dependable truck—a truck you can count on to deliver the goods right on the button, a truck that keeps going when the going's tough. That truck is Chevrolet!

Chevy trucks stay on the job and save on the job! They're rugged, pay their way with less downtime, more on-time deliveries, more stamina and durability. They help pay for their keep with super-efficient engines that give you penny-pinching gas mileage—plus the kind of power and performance you want and need on your job. America's most popular sixes for unsurpassed economy. V8's with longer life built into their compact, short-

stroke design. And Chevrolets pay off with modern cab features that add to safety and comfort . . . that help drivers stay on the ball and on time. Like High-Level ventilation and concealed Safety Steps.

Whatever your job . . . you save by being right on schedule. That's why every Chevrolet—from perky pickup to tough 36,000-lb. G.V.W. tandem—is designed and engineered to help you meet delivery dates dependably.

Talk to your Chevrolet dealer soon. He'll be happy to show you a truck for your job that gets to your job on time. . . . Chevrolet Division of General Motors, Detroit 2, Mich.

57-CH-70

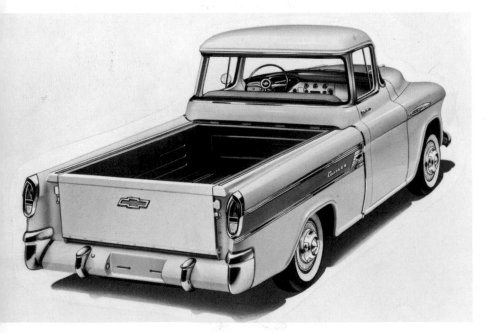

For the 1955 model year, all 5,220 Cameo Carriers were painted Bombay Ivory with Commercial Red accents, with a red bed and red-and-beige interior much like that of the upscale Chevrolet Bel Air. The trucks also had red three-spoke steering wheels, red floor mats, and full Bel Air–style wheel covers on ivory-colored rims.

During the 1956 model year, Chevrolet produced 1,452 Cameo Carriers. Bodysides and wheel covers got black accents, and the trucks were available in eight two-tone paint schemes, with three optional color combinations for the cabins.

ABOVE: An advertisement showcasing Chevy's 1957 truck lineup.

LEFT: A design sketch of the 1957 Cameo Carrier.

LEFT: The new face of the 1958 Cameo Carrier.

BELOW: To demonstrate the rugged durability of its new Task-Force family of trucks, Chevrolet would put a group of five of its trucks to the test on the rugged Alcan 'Highway' in Alaska. This is a sketch of what that trim might look like.

1958 was the final year for the Cameo Carrier.

Cameo Carriers got a chrome version of the Chevy pickup's new grille for 1957, as well as sculpted and wider trim along the bedsides featuring the "3124" model designation. A variation on the two-tone colors—inside and out—was again available on the 2,244 produced this year.

Like other 1958 Chevrolet pickups, the Cameo Carrier got dual headlamps for what would be its final year of production. This model year also brought a larger, 283-cid V-8 engine. Although fewer than fifteen hundred appeared, the Cameo Carrier's smoothed bedsides were reflected in the new Apache Fleetside pickup, which was built on the longer ¾-ton chassis, and featured a longer bed.

The Cameo Carrier design was influential beyond Chevy's own trucks: for 1957, Ford introduced its Styleside pickup design and Dodge offered its Sweptline styling.

"Though killed early in 1958, the Cameo was by no means a disappointment," Mueller notes, continuing:

Success in this case shouldn't be measured by sales figure or longevity; it is defined better by impact. Plainly put, the pickup market was never the same again after the Cameo's debut. Chevrolet had clearly demonstrated what a little (or a lot of) car-like class could do for pickup popularity.

The Cameo Carrier demonstrated the potential, and the Chevrolet product pipeline was about to deliver a pickup truck that took the car-like theme to a new extreme.

CONQUERING THE ALCAN

There's a road that lies under Northern skies
Toward the Land of the Midnight Sun,
It crosses the crest of the great Northwest
And it's known as the Alcan Run.
From Dawson's Creek with the Task-Force fleet of the '57 line,
We blaze the way for Chevrolet to conquer the Alcan grind . . .

So begins the narrative of a four-minute promotional movie Chevrolet produced as part of the launch of its Task-Force truck lineup for 1957. To showcase the strength and stamina of these trucks, Chevrolet sent a five-truck caravan on the rugged, unpaved Alcan Highway, driving from Dawson Creek in British Columbia north through Canada's Yukon Territory, and then on to Fairbanks in the middle of Alaska, nearly two years before it became a state.

The trucks included a Cameo Carrier, a one-ton panel truck with a double-axled dump body, a panel-bodied, low-cab forward vehicle, and a pair of big trailer-pulling tractors, one equipped with the Powermatic transmission. Each truck either carried or pulled the sort of load typical of its normal use.

After officials of the American Automobile Association (AAA) inspected and sealed the vehicles at the GM Proving Grounds in Michigan to verify they were examples of standard production, the Alcan Run was underway. They arrived at Dawson Creek, where the caravan vehicles were inspected and sealed by the AAA again before the drive to Fairbanks. From there, they looped back along the Alcan Highway to Dawson Creek, then on to Detroit, where they were again certified by the AAA.

Despite stormy weather that in some places turned the gravel and dirt road "to paste," the trucks reached Fairbanks to complete the 1,520-mile drive from Dawson Creek in just forty-five hours—a remarkable performance for a trip that usually took seventy-two hours in ideal conditions.

ABOVE: Chevy trucks proving their ruggedness on the Alcan Highway.

RIGHT: After the successful completion of the Alcan adventure, Chevrolet celebrated with a series of advertisements.

So we made our push through the Arctic bush
On that ribbon of mountainous road,
And we held our stride on the rugged ride
In spite of the heavy load.
Our 'matic transmission locked in position,
no shifting from drive to low,
Proving by test that Chevy is best
wherever a truck can go.
There were rivers to span with our caravan
and the valleys were wide and deep,
Though the way was hard,
with hydraulic retard,
we held where the grades were steep.
Statistics say
at the Triple A,
it's a 72-hour drive,
But we roared down
into Fairbanks town
in less than 45!
If you haul loads
over all kinds of roads,
Chevy trucks are No. 1.
They're engineered best
and proven by test:
The champs of the Alcan Run!

HERE! NEW TASK·FORCE 57 CHEVROLET TRUCKS
The fleet that conquered the Alcan Highway

Return of the Car-Based Pickup

Automakers work hard to anticipate customer needs, but sometimes all they have to do is to listen to their customers. Take, for example, a letter written in 1932 by the wife of an Australian farmer. Why, the woman asked, couldn't a truck be built that would be comfortable enough to carry people to church on Sunday but sturdy enough to carry pigs to market the rest of the week?

She addressed her request to the managing director of the Ford assembly plant in Geelong, located west of Melbourne on Port Phillip Bay, in the Australian state of Victoria. Soon, both General Motors' Australian affiliate, Holden, and Ford were producing such car-based vehicles (called "utes" in Australia), designed to carry people up front and livestock or produce in the bed.

For American automakers, it was a form of déjà vu, because the first pickups built by Chevrolet, Ford, Dodge, and others were also based on standard car chassis. Later, in the United States, automakers built what were called "coupe deliveries" or "business coupes," which were standard passenger cars that replaced the traditional trunk with a pickup-style bed.

For the 1959 model year, Chevrolet launched a ute-like vehicle designed for the American market and customer needs, the El Camino. With a name taken from Spanish for "the way," "the road," or "the journey," this new design was built on a sturdy station

wagon chassis. Based on the two-door version of Chevrolet's Brookwood station wagon—though dressed up by adding side trim from the upscale Bel Air sedan—the new El Camino was long, low, and stunning. The '59 Chevy's horizontal rear bat wings looked better behind a pickup truck than on the wagon, which gave the new vehicle a boost and provided Chevrolet dealers and their customers an even more stylish pickup than the earlier Cameo Carrier.

The standard powertrain in the El Camino was a 235-cubic-inch inline six-cylinder with a three-speed manual transmission. Two V-8 engines—a 250-horsepower, fuel-injected 283-cid and a 315-horsepower 348-cid topped by three carburetors—and Powerglide and Turboglide automatics were also available.

While Chevrolet introduced its new C and K, two-wheel drive and four-wheel drive, truck models for 1960, the '60 El Camino was again built on the passenger car–based station wagon. In addition to a new grille with "floating" headlamps and a more angular

OPPOSITE: The 1959 Chevrolet El Camino was new, but it also marked a return to the roots of the first car-based Chevrolet trucks.

El Camino was based on Chevrolet's Brookwood station wagon, with the roof removed from behind the front seats and a pickup-style bed installed.

overall design, the back end of the '60 El Camino had kinked, "gull-wing"-style horizontal fins.

But El Caminos cost several hundred dollars more than a brand-new, half-ton Apache pickup. After selling twenty-two thousand of the car-based trucks in 1959 and only fourteen thousand in 1960, Chevrolet decided to halt production and come back with something more fitting to customer needs.

"Chevrolet officials were regrouping, rethinking their position . . ." Mike Mueller writes in his book *Chevrolet Pickups*. "They didn't have anything else to work with, at least not until 1964, when General Motors' new A-body intermediates debuted."

Actually, Chevrolet did offer another car-based pickup while it rethought the El Camino. From 1961 through 1964, Chevrolet produced a pickup version of its rear-engined Corvair compact. Chevrolet introduced the Corvair as a coupe, sedan, and convertible in 1960 and, a year later, added van and pickup versions. Though its air-cooled six-cylinder engine provided only 80 horsepower, the Corvair 95 could be equipped with an innovative ramp-style "door" on the curb side. In standard pickup configuration, it was the Loadstar; with the side door, it was the Rampside.

Chevrolet was also working on its version of General Motors' new A-body cars. Known at the time as "intermediates," the A-bodies were larger than the compacts but smaller than the full-size vehicles. This model was the Chevelle, also appearing in an upscale version named for a popular Los Angeles beach community, Malibu.

For the 1964 model year, Chevrolet unveiled its Chevelle, with two- and four-door sedans and station wagons, and the Malibu, a sport coupe, sedan, convertible, and station wagon. The company also released the next-generation El Camino, based on the same new intermediate-sized passenger-car chassis. A standard El Camino had interior appointments similar to those in the Chevelle, while the El

ALL: An early running prototype for the El Camino lacks side trim and the cat's-eye taillamps that characterized 1959 production versions.

RIGHT: With its limited cargo-carrying capacity, the El Camino was seen as sort of a gentlemen's pickup truck.

BELOW: Long and low, El Camino was sexier than the station wagon on which it was based.

Camino Custom offered upscale Malibu-style accoutrements. Both versions had pickup boxes that widened from 59¾ inches behind the cab to 64¾ inches at the tailgate, with 46 inches between the wheel housings. The beds were 78½ inches long. Overall, the beds were larger than in 1959 and 1960, when the El Caminos were based on full-size cars.

The standard engine for the new El Camino was 120 horsepower, with a 194-cubic-inch six (a 140-horsepower, 230-cid Turbo-Thrift six was also available), while Custom versions sported a 195-horsepower, 283-cid V-8, or even a 250-horsepower 327. Options included a four-speed synchromesh gearbox, power brakes and steering, and a Positraction rear axle.

Like the Chevelle/Malibu on which it was based, El Camino underwent styling updates for the 1965 model year. Perhaps most significant was an updated options list that now included 300-, 350-, and even 375-horsepower versions of the 327-cid V-8.

Meanwhile, a Super Sport (SS) version of the Chevelle coupe and convertible was added to the passenger car lineup. Features included brightwork body trim, special badging, black-accented grille and rear cove, special wheel covers, bucket seats with bright trim, a center console, and special instrument cluster with temperature, ammeter, and oil pressure gauges. Added as a midyear option was the SS 396 model with dual exhaust, a four-speed manual shifter, tweaked suspension, mag-look wheel covers, AM/FM multiplex audio, and, most important, a 375-horsepower, 396-cubic-inch "big-block" V-8.

Another car-based Chevrolet pickup was the 1961 Corvair 95 Rampside, based on the van version of Chevrolet's compact, rear-engined car.

As Chevrolet launched its 1966 model year, the same equipment on the SS 396 (except for the badging) was available on El Camino, which also got new sheet metal, based on the redesign of the Chevelle/Malibu passenger car. That equipment also was optional for the 1967 El Camino, the last to be built on that first-generation Chevelle/Malibu foundation.

The SS 396 badging came on the El Camino for the 1968 model year, when the El Camino was based on the next-generation Chevelle/Malibu. That meant a slightly longer wheelbase, more streamlined styling—with a slightly smaller pickup bed—and even flying buttress B-pillars.

By the 1970 model year, the 396 engine was enlarged to 402 cid, though badging continued to read 396 because of the popularity and respect that number had earned. Midway through the 1970 model year, however, an even more powerful engine was offered in El Camino—Chevrolet's huge 454-cid V-8—in two versions, one pumping out 360 horsepower, the other 450. This made El Camino a true muscle machine during Detroit's muscle car heyday, reportedly capable of sprinting a quarter-mile in less than 13.5 seconds and reaching speeds of nearly 110 miles per hour in the process.

But that heyday was about to run up against oil embargoes and gas lines. The 454 engine option remained for 1971, but the engine was rated at only 425 gross horsepower that year, and then detuned to only 240 net horsepower

OPPOSITE: Rampside made a lot of chores easier to accomplish.

ABOVE AND FOLLOWING PAGE: The Corvair platform provided the possibility of adding a curbside ramp to ease access to cargo.

LEFT: The second generation of the Chevrolet El Camino ended with the 1967 model year. The SS carried a 396-cubic-inch V-8 that provided 350 horsepower.

ABOVE: In 1970, the third-generation El Camino SS offered a cowl-induction hood and as much as 450 horsepower when equipped with a 454-cubic-inch V-8 (the 396 version is shown here).

for 1972. Reacting to a changing world, Chevrolet launched a new light utility vehicle in 1972, the Chevy LUV, which was a mini pickup based on a Japanese vehicle built by Isuzu.

El Camino got new bodywork for 1973, plus Estate and SS trim packages: SS offered two-tone paint, while Estate appeared with faux-woodgrain trim.

The car-based truck rolled on, though in 1977 it received stacked headlamps (which were discontinued the following year). In 1978, Chevrolet launched a new Malibu with a slightly longer wheelbase. This meant that the next-gen El Camino rode on a 117.1-inch platform, though its overall length was slightly shorter; it also had single headlamps at either end of its grille, new quarter windows just

behind the seats, and a new standard V-6 engine (though rated at only 95 horsepower). The new El Camino also was 600 pounds lighter than the previous generation.

While El Caminos got a new 267-cid V-8 engine for 1979 in addition to the Royal Knight model, the big news for car-based trucks was that Ford would end production of its Ranchero model.

The Chevrolet SSR, which turned into an open roadster thanks to its power-retracting roof, could be equipped with a six-speed manual transmission.

El Camino, along with GMC's Caballero, would have the market to themselves for the next few years with regular styling updates, an optional 5.7-liter diesel engine in 1983, and a new V-6 in 1985. But the automotive marketplace was changing. People were moving to vehicles that could provide even more lifestyle options than a car-based truck—minivans and sport utility vehicles were the new rage. Four months into calendar year 1988, Chevrolet ended production of the El Camino model.

"Most dependable, longest lasting." That's the motto for Chevrolet trucks and, while they haven't been in production for nearly thirty years, the story of the El Camino proves those words. Car-based trucks continue to draw a cult following among collectors and enthusiasts, and a stunning number of them can still be seen on the road.

ABOVE: The El Camino was based on a late-'50s Chevrolet station wagon. In contrast, the SSR was based on the modern version of a station wagon, the SUV. Like the El Camino, though, it featured a pickup bed in the back.

RIGHT: Unlike the El Camino, the SSR had a retractable hardtop and turned into an open-top roadster.

SSR

Every so often, rumors emerge of the possibility of a successor to the seemingly evergreen El Camino. One oft-told story has had GM importing its Australian-built ute.

Soon after the turn of the twenty-first century, Chevrolet *did* launch a new car-like pickup that reminded many of the beloved El Camino. That new model was the Super Sport Roadster, or SSR.

Chevrolet dealerships sold these vehicles from the 2003 through the 2006 model years. Although based on the platform of a sport utility vehicle, the SSR looked as if it might be the grandchild of the El Camino—albeit with retro styling inspired by the Advanced-Design pickups of the postwar era.

The SSR, which even served one year as the official pace car for the Indianapolis 500-mile race, had a retractable hardtop that opened the cockpit into a roadster configuration to provide a topless driving experience.

At first, beneath the rounded, retro-styled hood was Chevrolet's 300-horsepower, 5.3-liter V-8 engine. Starting in 2005, that powerplant was replaced by the 390-horsepower LS2 V-8 derived from the Chevrolet Corvette (and, for 2006, horsepower bumped up to 400).

For all its power and performance potential, though, the SSR could carry only limited payload in its covered bed, and the base price of $42,000 put the SSR out of the reach of many people.

Nonetheless, even more than a decade after the last SSR rolled off the assembly line, there are those who still dream of a day when Chevrolet will offer another car-based pickup truck in sufficient volume that it makes business sense while meeting the needs and wants of its customers.

BELOW: Chevrolet introduced an El Camino for the new millennium with its SSR, short for Super Sport Roadster.

OPPOSITE: A hard tonneau covered the SSR's pickup bed. Meanwhile, its hood covered a powerful V-8 engine.

Recreational Opportunities

In 1960, two years before he received the Nobel Prize for Literature, author John Steinbeck decided to go "in search of America." He bought a brand-new, dark green GMC pickup truck, outfitted it with a customized, slide-in camper unit, named his steed Rocinante (after Don Quixote's horse), and, joined by his poodle, Charley, drove across the United States and back. This journey was the inspiration for his bestselling book Travels with Charley: In Search of America.

As it turned out, Steinbeck was at the leading edge of a trend: using pickup trucks for something other than workaday chores. The fact that the all-new 1960-model-year pickups from Chevrolet and GMC were sleeker, more stylish, and easier to drive certainly helped encourage this trend.

"By 1960 Average Joe, his family, and friends were finding themselves with more leisure time on their hands—as well as more disposable funds in their bank accounts—than ever before," Mike Mueller writes in *Chevrolet Pickups*. "Many middle-class mates began buying recreational toys: travel trailers, truck campers, and camping trailers."

Add in a growing fleet of newly purchased recreational boats that needed towing and, Mueller states, "It was the camping and boating craze more than any other fad, frenzy, or factor that helped feed the ever-growing truck market in the 1960s."

The market for pickups was growing, and quickly. In 1960, Chevrolet produced

nearly four-hundred thousand trucks, something it hadn't done since the pent-up postwar demand for trucks in 1950. By 1963, Chevrolet's truck production had topped 480,000. A year later, its production surpassed half a million, and then exceeded six-hundred thousand the following year. That year, 1965, also was the first time overall light-truck sales in the United States surpassed the one million mark.

This was a watershed moment for Chevrolet. In 1965, more than half of the more than nine million Chevrolet trucks ever built—and that figure dates back to at least 1918!—were still still registered and on the road in 1965.

To feed this growing demand for pickup trucks, Chevrolet rolled out its next generation of such vehicles for the 1960 model year. These trucks were so new—and so different—that they even came with new nomenclature.

For the 1960 model year, Chevrolet produced 185 trucks on eighteen wheelbases. Except for the car-based El Camino, the various trucks

OPPOSITE: A 1960 Chevrolet Apache C10 loaded for market.

were identified by letters and numbers, and, in some cases by a model name as well.

The standard pickup trucks were either C (for conventional rear-wheel drive) or K (for those with factory-installed four-wheel drivetrains, which Chevrolet had begun building for the 1957 model year). Chevrolet also produced P, L, S, and M trucks; S, for example, was short for chassis designed to carry school bus bodies, while M signified a truck with tandem rear axles. Further, letters were followed by a number indicating the truck's load-carrying capacity, such as

C10 (a half-ton), C20 (three-quarter ton), C30 (one ton), or C40 (1.5 ton).

Apache was carried over as the name for light-duty trucks, which were available with Stepside or Fleetside panels on the outside of their pickup beds, with solid panels or as windowed Carryall Suburban wagon-style bodywork, or as a Step Van. Heavier-duty trucks also were available in Stake and Step Van configurations.

The styling of the new Chevrolet C/K pickup trucks was longer, lower, and strongly inspired by the jet age.

The leading edge of the hood in these trucks featured what almost looked like flared nostrils, which were actually copied from the jet pod air intakes on new military aircraft. The hood appeared to bulge over the front fenders, a design theme carried back through the doors and top edge of the pickup bed. When optioned with two-tone paint, the entire truck above that narrowed waistline was painted a contrasting color to more fully accentuate the new styling.

Though the design of this new generation of pickup trucks was the most obvious change, the big news lay beneath the revised sheet metal.

Wheelbases grew by 1 (C10) to 3¾ (C20) inches. Cabins were wider (with an extra 5.8 inches of seating width) and longer, providing more leg- and headroom even though the rooflines were a whopping seven inches lower!

Lower, because the new C/K trucks featured a new cabin affixed to a new and stronger frame with a lowered X-member. Access into this lowered cabin was much easier and removed the need for the steps built into the cabins of earlier Task-Force trucks. Even with a lower roofline, the new cabins were larger and more comfortable, and the new frame also lowered the trucks' center of gravity to improve handling, particularly because it enabled perhaps the biggest change of all—a new independent front suspension.

Chevrolet brochures at the time announced that the new suspension "does more for you than any other single feature ever introduced!"

Gone were "friction-producing front leaf springs. Instead, each front wheel is suspended independently of the other . . . Tough-steel

BELOW AND FOLLOWING PAGE: The Apache C10 was ready for work or play.

ABOVE: This 1960 Chevrolet pickup is an Apache K10 with four-wheel drive.

torsion bars assist the rugged control arms and low-friction spherical joints in providing precise wheel action and a new kind of truck springing."

The ride had become so smooth, the brochure said, that it has to be experienced to be believed.

"And it's just as tough as it is smooth!"—this was thanks to rigid control arms, sturdier frames, torsion bar springs, and low-friction linkage (ball-and-socket joints linking axles to wheels).

Further, brochures of this period noted that the trucks' rear suspensions had been "tailored" to work with the new independent front setups. These featured frictionless coil springs on Series 10 and 20 models, new springs on Series 30 and 40 models, new variable-rate leafs on Series 50, 60, 70, and 80 trucks, and even new high-capacity tandem suspensions for trucks with dual rear axle architecture.

Mueller notes that the new setup:

traded the traditional (and obsolete) I-beam axle and parallel leaves for a car-style independent arrangement featuring upper and lower A-arms. Yet another concession to the civilization of the American pickup, independent front

This Chevrolet Apache 10 Carryall Suburban shares its styling with the Chevrolet pickup trucks that launched the new design for the 1960 model year.

suspension (IFS) also improved ride by minimizing road shocks and smoothing out bumps. The 1959's solid front axle suspended by leaf springs sent those jars and jumps directly to the seat of the driver's pants. Stability was also compromised, as whenever one front wheel rode up over a bump, so too did that corner of the truck. The IFS allowed each front wheel to absorb shocks separately, and suspension travel translated far less into vertical frame movements.

"Independent front suspension represented another major milestone for the Chevrolet pickup," Mueller concludes, calling the new suspension "ground-breaking," with additional "cutting-edge" technology in the form of modern ball-joints instead of old-fashioned kingpins, thus enhancing steering control.

In his multipart history of Chevrolet trucks for pickuptrucks.com, Don Bunn writes that the new independent front suspension with torsion bars was used on all new C/K trucks, except for those with four-wheel drive and on forward-

BOTH: After only two years, Chevrolet redesigned its trucks for the 1962 model year. The Apache name was dropped, as was the nostril-style hood. A new front end also featured single headlamps. This mockup of the new Stepside version was photographed at the GM design center in the summer of 1961.

control models. He adds that rear springs were coils on 10 (half-ton) and 20 (three-quarter ton) models while 30 (one-ton) trucks retained rear leaf springs.

With the El Camino on hiatus, Chevrolet launched two Corvair-based pickups, the Corvair 95 in Loadside and Rampside configurations, for the 1961 model year (there was also a Corvair-based van, the Corvan). Chevrolet called the new Corvair-based trucks a "totally new concept in light-duty trucking."

C and K pickups of this period were little changed beyond cosmetics, though they did get foam-rubber seat cushioning, and three more versions were equipped with four-wheel drive.

A Chevrolet brochure bragged that C/K buyers could get "more work done in a day,"

because the independent suspension—"floating ride"—meant faster schedules on any road surface. It also noted that maintenance costs were reduced because a jolt-free ride meant less wear and tear on parts.

"Owners' earning power began to soar [with the new truck for the 1960 model year] and word got around," the brochure proclaimed.

The Apache name disappeared from C/K trucks after the 1961 model year; also gone was the jet-pod hood design. Two years later, coil springs replaced the torsion bars on C/K trucks, and a new egg-crate style grille became part of their profile; also new for the 1963 model year was a short-stroke, 230-cubic-inch that replaced the larger, heavier, Stovebolt 6, which had become outdated.

A new El Camino launched for the 1964 model year. It was the last year for Corvair-based trucks, although Chevrolet did roll out its G Van for 1965.

More significant for typical truck buyers, however, was new sheet metal for the C/K vehicles. Gone was the wraparound windshield; instead, A-pillars were canted rearward, vent windows were wider at the bottom than the top, and door openings themselves were widened as well, making egress even easier.

There was big news for 1965 with the installation of Chevrolet's touted 327-cubic-inch small-block V-8 in the C/K trucks. Also available was factory-installed air conditioning, and several federally mandated safety features arrived as well.

Though it would be at least a decade or two before the do-it-yourself craze would hit and people would look at pickup trucks as necessities for suburban living, the trucks themselves were ready for this revolution, thanks to all the new equipment being installed. Trucks were still capable of even the most severe of workaday chores for those in the trades, in farming and ranching, and in other fields where strong, hard-working, and long-lasting trucks were a necessity, but at the same time they were becoming more civilized and ready for a new and emerging set of owners.

Chevrolet offered a Camper Special package (RPO Z81) for 327-equipped C20 trucks that added a thicker front stabilizer bar, heavy-duty rear shocks, auxiliary rear springs, larger tires and exterior mirrors, two-speed windshield wipers, upgraded heater/defroster unit, radio, and dual sun visors. The trade publication *Automotive News* reported that the reason the C/K vehicles were

A couple of the new-for-1962 Chevrolet Fleetside pickups.

getting the 327 V-8 was "to meet the needs of the booming recreation vehicle market."

"All the customer had to do was slip in the camper of his choice and go whenever he wanted, confident that he had bought the right truck for the job—make that adventure—at hand," Mueller adds.

Just as it had in 1957 when it sent a fleet of its trucks to the Arctic Circle, Chevrolet demonstrated the durability and dependability of its trucks with a 1963 trip down Mexico's Baja Peninsula and back.

"Baked . . . Battered . . . Abused," proclaimed advertising related to the drive. The trip

ABOVE: A 1962 Chevrolet half-ton pickup with four-wheel drive.

RIGHT: A 1963 Chevrolet C-10 at a work site.

CHEVY TRUCK LEGENDS: RESURRECTED '64 C10

When he was a teenager, Gary "Scooter" McClendon had a 1964 Chevrolet C10 short-bed pickup truck.

"I loved it," he said. "[So, many years later], I tried to resurrect one just like it and ended up with a much better one."

Eventually, that is. McClendon's hunt for a truck like the one he'd owned in his youth took him to a Texas automotive graveyard, where he found a '64 C10, or at least the fifty-some pieces of one that it would take him two years to put back together into a working vehicle.

McClendon's truck has traveled more than half a million miles since it was new, and continues to carry him to and from work—nearly 35 miles from his home—on nearly a daily basis.

Part of the reason that he drives his vintage Chevy so often is that he also has a newer vehicle that he doesn't want to wear out prematurely! Most dependable, longest-lasting trucks on the road, indeed.

featured half a dozen trucks, ranging from a couple of C10s—one with a camper mounted into its bed—to a diesel tanker and a dumper with double rear axles. It began in Michigan, went north and west, then down the West Coast to the tip of the Mexican peninsula, then back north, across the border, and finally northeast across the southern-tier states toward home.

"On Mexico's barren Baja California Peninsula, a caravan of six 1963 Chevrolet trucks withstood 2,000 miles of grueling punishment on the toughest performance challenge imaginable—the Baja Run!" a brochure proclaimed.

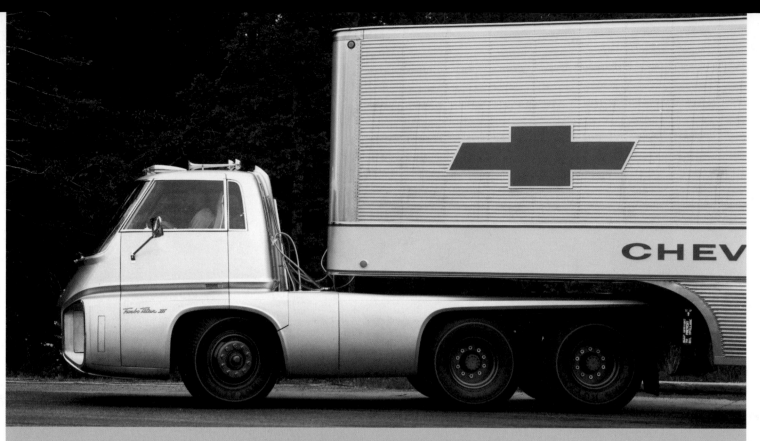

CONCEPT TRUCKS

Automakers frequently create concept cars that point the way (they hope) to our automotive future. Much less frequently, they produce truck concept vehicles.

Today, Chevrolet regularly previews concept trucks at the SEMA show in Las Vegas. Many ultimately make it into production—this includes the Midnight, the High Desert, and the Alaskan Edition. Some are, at least for the time of this writing, pure concept trucks, such as the Carhartt edition.

One of the very first Chevrolet truck concepts included the 1959 Palomino, designed by Chuck Jordan, who had styled the Cameo Carrier pickup.

There was the Golden Cameo, a 1967 pickup truck with hidden headlights and an SS emblem on its grille, built to tow the Golden Camaro concept as part of the Golden Anniversary of Chevrolet truck sales in 1968.

More recently, there was the 1989 Chevrolet XT-2 concept, looking like a Camaro-based El Camino, that was part of the PPG-sponsored Indycar racing series pace car fleet.

Of all of these, the most iconic, classic Chevrolet concept truck fleet was 1966's Turbo-Titan III.

The Turbo-Titan III wasn't a pickup truck, but a vision for a future—and futuristic—semi-tractor, complete with a custom-built 40-foot stainless-steel trailer. Cab and trailer stretched only 50 feet in length, but the rig had an operating gross combined weight rating of 76,800 pounds.

The cab's design was radical, to say the least. Made from steel and fiberglass, the truck had retractable, square-lens headlamps stacked three on each side and housed in the same frame as the air inlets for the turbine engine. Turn signals were located in retractable housings that disappeared when not in use to smooth airflow around the cab.

In the cab were a pair of "astronaut seats," an array of gauges much like an airplane's, and a twin-dial steering system on a pedestal that could be moved fore and aft for driver comfort. The truck was among the first vehicles to include a portable telephone.

Propelling the truck was the fifth-generation gas turbine engine developed by General Motors. The fuel-efficient engine was rated at 280 horsepower with 875 pound-feet of torque—at idle.

Though the Turbo-Titan III didn't go into production, the effort enhanced Chevrolet's knowledge of alternative powerplants and fuels, as well as providing a practical demonstration of how design could be an effective way to improve fuel economy.

ABOVE: In 1966, Chevrolet unveiled its Turbo-Titan III, a concept for how the over-the-road semi-style truck of the future might appear. The truck and trailer were designed to be aerodynamic and fuel efficient.

As tough as the Alcan drive had been, the brochure gushed about the challenges faced by the 1963 tour:

[N]ever before has a new-truck producer gone to such lengths to show the stuff it's made of. So difficult was the going that the convoy seldom averaged more than 10 miles per hour for a day's travel (in Baja). The design and dependability of every truck component were put to the severest test as the new Chevies kept up a steady pace through boulder fields, cactus jungles, hub-deep sand, over burning-hot dry lake beds and up seemingly endless grades that rose from sea level to altitudes of more than 5,000 feet.

From Tijuana to Cabo San Lucas and back again, they maintained a steady pace over rocky grades, through sinking sand and choking dust; fought ever mile over a route that challenged every truck component. And *all* trucks in the caravan completed the Run and return to Detroit in good working order—logged more than 8,000 miles in a dramatic demonstration of the new reliability inherent in '63 Chevrolet truck design.

Roads or no . . . these trucks go.

Once again, Chevrolet had proven the durability and dependability of its trucks on a grueling road trip, and not only had they driven around the United States, but from the Arctic Circle to the tip of Mexico's Baja peninsula. Chevrolet had proven that its trucks could go places where other trucks feared to tread, but of equal importance Chevrolet was simultaneously preparing another generation of trucks that could meet the needs not only of hard-working construction teams and ranchers, but also those of an urban population that used trucks for commuting and recreation.

ABOVE: One aerodynamic feature of the Turbo-Titan III was the way its headlights were hidden when not in use.

BELOW: From its nose to the tail end of the trailer, the Turbo-Titan III concept stretched only 50 feet, shorter than most of today's semi trailers.

Trucks Can Be Glamorous

For the 1967 model year, Chevrolet rolled out new trucks with what it called "the most significant cab and sheet metal styling change in Chevrolet history." "Beneath that never-before-seen truck appearance there's a whole new build that means more durability, comfort, working ease and safety!" the sales brochure proclaimed.

"The new styling represents the most extensive Chevrolet truck configuration change since 1960," wrote A. C. Mair, the director of Chevrolet truck engineering, who noted that the company was producing 406 standard truck models on thirty-seven wheelbases. These represented an increase of sixty-seven versions and two wheelbases compared to the company's domestic truck fleet for 1966.

"Numerous product improvements are incorporated," he continued, "adding to Chevrolet's tradition of greater value, reliability, and variety for its customers."

He seemed particularly proud of the way the design and engineering changes had lowered the stance of the four-wheel-drive K versions of Chevrolet's new generation of trucks. The two-wheel-drive C models were nearly two inches longer and more than two inches lower, while four-wheel-driven K versions were more than 4½ inches lower, still retaining the same ramp breakover angles to diminish off-pavement travel.

The interior width of truck beds on Fleetside

pickups was reduced by some 2½ inches, but they still stretched more than five feet across. Load capacity for these models was enhanced by a new flat-topped design for the rear wheel housings, which protruded into the bed.

Mair also noted that, for 1967, Chevrolet trucks were equipped with a long list of new safety features, including padded instrument panels and sunshades, four-way hazard warning flashers, safety door locks and hinges, laminated windshield glass, a dual master-cylinder brake system with dashboard warning light, telescoping lower steering shaft, and energy-absorbing steering wheels.

"Good continuity of line and a less massive appearance are evident in the new body and sheet metal styling," a Chevrolet truck engineering brochure noted. "The flat, sloping hood, new integrated grille panel, and lower overall height—especially on Four-Wheel Drive models—also enhance vehicle appearance."

The Standard Catalog of Chevrolet Trucks entry for these trucks is considerably more effusive:

OPPOSITE: Though more glamorous in styling, Chevrolet trucks remained fully capable of any sort of work or terrain they might be asked to take on.

In 1967, Chevrolet applied what at the time it called the "most significant" change of cab and sheet metal styling in company history. The styling was updated, but many product improvements were added to make the truck more valuable, reliable, and versatile for its buyers.

The new styling reflected the importance of an attractive appearance in the light-duty truck field, as more and more were purchased for personal transportation and camper use.

The major styling themes on the Pickup combined an inner slant above the belt line with a side body feature line nearly dividing the wheelwells into equal sections. A new lower cab with increased glass area featured a new rigid roof designed for extra strength.

The front end was very attractive with single headlights recessed into square receptacles at either end of a grille with a single wide center bar.

Chevrolet truck historian Don Bunn called the generation of 1967–1972 the "Glamour" pickups. The idea of a pickup truck being glamorous may be in the eye of the beholder, but the new design certainly has withstood the test of time and the trucks of this period are highly favored by today's classic car (and truck) collectors, as well as by hot rodders.

To feed the need for more glamour, even in pickup trucks, Chevrolet offered the Custom Sport Truck option package (RPO Z84) for the 1967 model year. The package covered heavy-truck pickups in addition to C/K10 models. Available only in Fleetside architecture, the Custom Sport Truck option package included a chromed front bumper, brightwork exterior trim—including silver anodized grille background—carpeting, chromed switchgear knobs, brightwork trim on pedals, and a center armrest with a built-in storage compartment.

That center armrest could be pivoted upright to provide a third seat since the Custom Sport Truck option included bucket seats for the first time in a Chevrolet pickup truck.

More than twelve thousand customers opted for the Custom Sport Truck package in 1967, a figure that swelled to nearly thirty thousand buyers by the 1969 model year. But even without the optional Custom Sport Truck, the new generation of Chevrolet pickups offered a more comfortable cabin, with lower step-in and even air conditioning.

(Continued on page 111)

The Chevrolet Sport Truck was a special option package that included a chromed front bumper, bright exterior trim, carpeted interior, a pivoting center armrest, and the first bucket seats available (but not shown here) in a Chevy pickup.

Even deep down inside, Chevrolet is the best built pickup you can buy.

Tough, truck-built coil springs at all four wheels give a road-balanced ride with solid comfort.

Chevrolet Independent Front Suspension stops bumps where they start, adds to long truck life.

Extra-strong double-wall construction in Fleetside cargo body stands up to the toughest jobs.

Sheet metal is engineered with a reduced number of external joints, less chance of rust.

½-ton CST Fleetside Pickup

Double-strong cab has double walls of sheet metal in many areas to stay tight, quiet and strong.

Only Chevrolet gives you all this deep down value

... exclusive front and rear coil springs, double walls of sheet metal in vital areas, rust-resistant design, biggest choice of engines of any popular pickup. And a lot more.

Chevrolet's extra value is not always out where you can see it. But it adds up to *inner strength* ... makes a Chevy pickup the strong, silent type that does more work for your dollar.

When you've worked a Chevy on many a tough job, in good weather and bad, over back roads and superhighways ... you'll begin to see what we mean. . . . Chevrolet Division of General Motors, Detroit, Michigan.

CHEVROLET *Job Tamer* **pickups**

Special fender liners up front are self-washing. Rust-causing elements just can't find a foothold.

Half-ton Fleetside CST Pickup   Half-ton Stepside Pickup

A Chevy pickup is built to be womanhandled.

Don't get us wrong. Mankind's favorite truck is as tough as ever. It's got double-wall steel in all the vital areas. More power than any other popular pickup. And a rugged frame underneath.
But the '69 Chevy has womankind in mind, too. There's the smooth full coil spring ride, for example. And soft molded foam seats. Plus all the extras you can order, from power steering to air conditioning. It's enough to make the grade with any gal—or any guy who works, or camps, in a truck.
The '69 Chevy pickup is a lot more truck for a lot more people. As you and your spouse will agree, when you visit your Chevrolet dealer's.... Chevrolet Division of General Motors, Detroit, Mich.

More trucks are Chevrolets because Chevrolet is more truck!

OPPOSITE: This ad was part of a series promoting the late '60s Chevy pickups as "Job Tamer" trucks.

ABOVE: No longer limited to the work site, Chevrolet also touted the fact that its trucks were ready to be "womanhandled."

Compare a Chevy pickup's styling, ride, toughness and economy? With what?

Let's say you're about to buy a new pickup for business, recreation or both.

For years, more people have compared makes and then decided to buy a Chevrolet.

They took at Chevy styling. Boldly handsome for '69. But without that beast-of-burden look that's still around, even today.

Then there's ride. Only Chevrolet, of the popular pickups, has road-smoothing Independent Front Suspension with work-designed coil springs plus rear coils on most models.

Don't expect to find the toughness of Chevrolet's full-depth, double-wall Fleetside cargo box in just any pickup. There's double-wall strength in Chevy cabs, too.

Like most pickup owners, you'll find that the only pickup to compare with a Chevy is another Chevy pickup. So you have just one stop to make. Your Chevrolet dealer's. . . . Chevrolet Division of General Motors, Detroit, Mich.

Chevy has the lowest priced pickup with 8-ft. box of any popular make you can buy. And efficient Chevrolet engines that use regular grade gas extend those savings throughout the longer life of a Chevy pickup.

Chevrolet is more truck . . . day in, day out, day off!

RIGHT: This Chevrolet Sport Truck is among those that introduced bucket seats to the Chevrolet pickup truck lineup.

(Continued from page 107)

Those buying their trucks for camping could order both the Custom Sport Truck package and the Custom Camper package, which included upgraded suspension, wheels, and tires. Custom Campers were available in half-, three-quarter-, and one-ton trucks.

K series trucks equipped with four-wheel drive were lower because engineers had redesigned several parts of the powertrain and mounted the transfer case directly to the transmission; this provided for a higher position within the truck's undercarriage.

With the transfer case moved up within the undercarriage, the lowered truck still had some 12½ inches of clearance above the roadway.

Four-wheel-drive pickups also got power steering for the first time in 1967. But the big news lay hidden away.

"There's a lot more here than meets the eye," the 1967 sales brochure noted.

For example, some big advances in the battle against rust.

In 1971, Chevrolet became the first automaker to install front disc brakes on all of its light-duty pickup trucks, including this Cheyenne Fleetside.

Horses are great, but
sometimes you need a
full-size pickup truck.

New one-piece outer body side panels, with wrap-around ends do away with coach joints, a favorite attack point for corrosion. Rust-causing tire splash can't get up into the fender wells and other sheet metal any more either. It rolls right off the new bathtub-style fender skirts that surround the tires and protect the under carriage.

Durability also was further enhanced by another new feature: "Something new has been added to the all-steel pickup box too: full-depth double-wall side panels and tailgate. Keeps cargo dents from getting through to the outside wall."

The basic engine was a 250-cubic-inch straight six, a 292-cid six, a 283-cid V-8, and a 220-horsepower, 327-cid V-8. Six-cylinder engines were more popular with Chevy truck buyers, but 1967 was the last year this was the case. As Chevrolet celebrated its fiftieth anniversary as a truck producer, customers expressed with their pocketbooks, and for the first time over the course of a full model year, a strong preference for V-8s, and by a huge margin—more than 410,000 sold, compared to sales of fewer than 270,000 sixes.

Responding to customer needs, Chevrolet offered three new versions of its 350-cubic-inch small-block V-8 for the 1969 model year. They provided a choice of 255, 300, or 350 horsepower, based on compression ratio and carburetor configuration.

The last year of the decade was also the model year in which Chevrolet added the K Blazer, a compact sport utility vehicle, to its truck lineup.

While some customers needed more power, some had other needs—smaller, more fuel-efficient pickup trucks—and, in the early 1970s, Chevrolet developed something to meet those needs as well.

TOP: Rounded wheel openings were last part of the Chevrolet pickup truck design in the 1972 model year.

LEFT: This early 1970s proposal for a redesign of Chevrolet pickup trucks shows a split grille and squared fender wells. The grille remained a designer's dream, but the wheel wells went into production for the 1973 model year.

Pickups Sized for the Times

For the 1972 model year, Chevrolet introduced a small truck, its first compact truck. Like the vehicle itself, the truck's name was abbreviated: LUV, short for "light utility vehicle." It was an import produced by Tokyo-based Isuzu Motors.

Developed as the Isuzu KB as part of the Japanese-market pickup fleet—and sold in many export markets as the Isuzu Fasster—the 1972 LUV rode on a 102.4-inch wheelbase and featured a 1,100-pound payload rating, a heavy-duty frame, independent front and leaf spring rear suspension, and a cast-iron four-cylinder engine that provided 75 horsepower. First-year sales were slightly more than twenty-one thousand, but that figure grew to more than a hundred thousand by the end of a decade marked by oil crises, including the 1973 oil embargo and the so-called "oil shock" in 1979. The establishment of a national 55-mile-per-hour speed limit also served to diminish energy consumption, making fuel efficiency more attractive to the consumer.

The LUV was thirteen inches shorter than the foundation beneath the full-size Chevrolet C10 pickup. Overall length was 173.8 inches, more than two feet shorter than the C10. Despite its small stature, the little truck had a bed that was slightly more than six feet long and five feet wide.

The LUV received an automatic transmission option for the 1976 model year. The following year, it could be ordered as a chassis truck designed for a mini-motorhome, or in platform or stake-truck setups. Also offered was the "Mighty Mike" version with a racing-style stripe, white-spoke wheels, and wide, white-letter tires.

In 1978, the LUV was offered with a longer wheelbase (117.9) and 7 ½-foot bed. The mini-truck available in 1979 could be equipped with four-wheel drive—and sales of this model surpassed one hundred thousand.

A slightly more powerful 80-horsepower engine powered the LUV for 1980, when a Sport package was an option. In 1981, new bodywork featured more aerodynamic styling and an interior with 2½ more inches of legroom, among other updates. But sales fell off to 23,304 that year, as Chevrolet launched its first true homegrown compact truck, the S-10.

"There's Never Been a Truck Like It Before," read the banner on the brochure for the new S-10, a vehicle that was available in upgraded Tahoe, Durango, and Sport trim.

OPPOSITE: For Chevrolet's mini truck, it was LUV as well as "love."

A new-size American pickup. Chevrolet welcomes you to the future in pickups: the Chevy S-10. A high-mileage truck designed and assembled in America. A high-mileage truck with both a standard L4 and an optional V-6 engine... No imported pickup offers both a standard L4 and an optional V-6.

Linked to a four-speed manual gearbox, the four-cylinder engine—an 82-horsepower, 1.9-liter sourced from Isuzu nicknamed "Hustle"—was rated at 28 miles per gallon in city driving and at 39 on the highway, while the V-6—a 110-horsepower 2.8 liter produced by GM and nicknamed "Muscle"—was rated at 24 city and 34 highway. The V-6 also provided 148 pound-feet of torque, with peak power delivered at just 2,000 rpm.

In addition to its two engines choices, the S-10 offered two wheelbase options: 108.3 or 117.9 inches. The shorter version provided a 73-inch bed while the longer truck's bed stretched out to a full 89 inches. Payload ratings ranged from a standard 1,000 pounds to 1,500 when the V-6 was equipped with a heavy-duty package that included front stabilizer bar, heavy-duty rear springs, and power brakes.

A Heavy-Duty Trailering Package provided 4,000 pounds of towing capacity—"twice as much as any import."

"Stretch out, America," a brochure suggested as it pointed out the roomy dimensions of the compact truck's cabin. When it came to options, "no import offers so many," from halogen headlamps to cruise control, from a sliding rear window to power locks and windows, and from a cargo-cover cap for securing a load in the bed to styled wheels.

It may have been a compact truck, but the Chevrolet LUV was right sized—in dimensions, in dollars spent, and in fuel used—to meet the needs of many people.

Even the S-10's paint was special. While the typical American truck had three layers over its sheet metal, the S-10 had "a history-making finish," with the sheet metal covered by a layer of zinc phosphate, another of Elpo primer, then the actual primer, a chip-resistant coating for lower side panels, and the topcoat.

The actual assembly of the truck was new as well, according to the sales brochure.

The new Chevy S-10 is built in a special way. The front end, cab and pickup box are first computer-welded into separate units before being fitted to the frame. The S-10 is designed to be put together only one way: the correct way. If any of those and other assemblies don't fit, they are rejected. They are not simply adjusted to fit.

World's best-loved sport utility now comes with four doors. • Biggest V6 engine you can buy. • Standard 4-wheel anti-lock brakes. • Shift-on-the-fly Insta-Trac.™ America's favorite 4x4 system.

Chevy S-10 Blazer. Four-door, 4x4. Go where you want to go. Do what you want to do. Whenever you want to. That's the freedom Chevy S-10 Blazer offers. With its big V6 engine, 4-wheel anti-lock brakes, available seating for six and plenty of cargo room, you get confidence and convenience. So go ahead. Get in your Chevy S-10 Blazer. And charge.

More People Are Winning With **The Heartbeat** *of America.* **TODAY'S TRUCK IS CHEVROLET.**

ABOVE: The LUV was available in many colors.

LEFT: In 1983, Chevrolet introduced a sport utility vehicle that combined the size and strength of its compact S-10 pickup truck with the security of a roofed cargo area, as well as room for six people.

OPPOSITE: The Chevrolet LUV was redesigned for the 1981 model year with enhanced aerodynamics and a larger cabin.

ABOVE: Coming or going, the S-10 provided a reasonably sized, just-right pickup truck for many owners.

RIGHT: The Chevrolet Blazer shared its underpinnings, including its 4x4 drivetrain, with the S-10 compact pickup truck.

The result was "uncanny quality."

And everyone involved—factory workers, engineers, management, suppliers, everyone from design to assembly—"is part of its impressive quality story. The S-10 is a work of industry, science, art and love. It has comfort, high mileage and that unmistakable something only human genius and hard work can produce: Quality."

In 1983, the S-10 spawned the T-10, built on a four-wheel-drive chassis, and the S-10 Blazer sport utility vehicle. The 2.5-liter four-cylinder engine was updated, and Chevrolet made its 2.8-liter V-6 available in the compact trucks and SUV as well. The four provided 92 horsepower while the six offered 125, plus 150 pound-feet of torque.

Soon, the S-10 pickups could be purchased with an extended cab. Also available was an optional 4.3-liter "Vortex" V-6 good for 150 horsepower and, more importantly, 230 pound-feet of torque.

Of more than a half-million Chevrolet light-truck sales during the 1988 model year, the S and T compact pickups represented nearly half of all sales, around 250,000.

In 1989, Chevrolet resurrected a heralded nameplate, Cameo, for a special edition for the S-10. The special components included a wraparound front bumper, foglamps, flared

Chevrolet was the first US automaker to offer its own compact pickup when it launched the S-10.

ABOVE: By 1988, the S-10 was available with extended cab architecture.

RIGHT: Chevrolet continues to use the LUV badging on a compact pickup produced in Colombia.

wheelwells over ground-effects-style bodyside moldings, a flush-fitting tailgate, rear roll pan, and special badging. Apple Red, Frost White, and Midnight Black monotone colors were the only treatments available for the Cameo.

Also new for 1989 were standard anti-lock brakes on the S-10 rear wheels.

The first-generation S-10 continued in production through the 1993 model year, with other updates including shift-on-the-fly for four-wheel drive and a five-speed Getrag transmission.

The second-generation S-10—in two- and four-wheel-drive pickup trucks and Blazer SUV architecture—was introduced for the 1994 model year and stayed in production for a decade.

"They were all-new, from the inside out, with more power, more room, more precision, and more safety enhancements than ever before offered in this compact model," notes *The Standard Catalog*.

New special editions included the S-10 Super Sport and the T-10 ZR2. The SS had a 195-horsepower "enhanced Vortec" V-6 and

ZR2 was the special off-road setup for the Chevrolet S-10.

rode on a sport suspension with heavy-duty shocks, front stabilizer bar, 15-inch wheels, and lower-profile tires. The ZR2 off-road package came with a wider (by nearly four inches) track, 31-inch tires, a front air dam with built-in tow hooks, and a beefed-up rear axle.

By 1996, extended-cab versions got a third door to ease access to the rear seating area. Three years later, the trucks were updated inside and out and, instead of SS, the higher-performance S-10 was called the Xtreme. A crew cab was available in 2001, though it only offered four-wheel-drivetrain.

Isuzu had supplied the LUV to Chevrolet in the 1970s. Beginning in 1996, the Japanese company began selling a modified version of the US-built S-10 as the Isuzu Hombre pickup in South America.

In 2003, Chevrolet launched a small front-drive pickup in Latin America, badged as either the Chevrolet Montana or Chevrolet Tornado. The little trucks were powered by either a 1.4- or 1.8-liter four-cylinder engine. The trucks were produced in Brazil and also in South Africa, where they were called the Chevrolet Utility Bakkie. A second-generation version was introduced in 2011, with a third-gen following in 2016.

Meanwhile, for 2004, Chevrolet launched a new-size pickup truck. Larger than the compact S-10 it was replacing, but smaller than the full-size Silverado, this was the midsize Colorado.

According to Chevrolet:

Colorado will redefine the standard for the mid-size pickup truck segment by offering an unexpected combination of features that provide increased functionality and capability. Colorado is more than just a tough truck. It was crafted with a healthy dose of distinctive style and refinement.

Not just an 8/10s-scale Silverado, "It sits on its own distinct body-on-frame platform, and from its inception was conceived to be the best mid-size truck on the road." The chief engineer, Tom Wallace, pointed to exceptional ride and handling and to a new series of inline engines—including a five-cylinder rated at 220 horsepower and 225 pound-feet of torque. In both that engine and the four-cylinder, peak torque was available at 1,400 rpm or less.

Chevrolet's promotional materials described other selling points for the new vehicles, along with why they would catch the attention of new buyers:

While Colorado is bigger than the vehicles it replaces in Chevy's lineup, it is by no means intended to steal from the full-size segment. These are different trucks, meeting different needs, and targeted at a different buyer.

That buyer is a younger, more diverse customer. Colorado was not designed to appeal to the full-size pickup intender, but to the customer who needs a mid-size pickup. It is ready, willing and able to meet the specific needs of an entirely different type of truck buyer, the buyer who doesn't need the higher payloads, towing capacities and expenses of owning a full-size pickup.

Marketing Manager Janet Eckhoff called the Colorado "a personal-use truck for singles, couples or families who want more out of their mid-size pickups, but who still share one thing in common: Any truck they drive had better be 'a real truck.'"

In 2002, American buyers could equip their crew cab S-10s with the ZR5 package, which included a roof rack, wheel flares, side steps, and other features.

ALL: The S-10 nameplate continues in production in South America and other overseas markets, where it continues to be the right-sized vehicle for local needs.

And the Colorado was real, indeed. In fact, it would serve as the basis for the rugged Hummer H3.

While not designed to compete with the Silverado, Chevrolet noted that, "Colorado looks and feels more like a spacious, well-appointed full-size pickup than a typical mid-size truck. It brings a new level of comfort and capability to the segment, with craftsmanship and attention to detail evident throughout."

Midsize truck buyers wanted room in their trucks' cabins. The extended or four-door crew cab architecture was purchased by 80 percent of buyers. Colorado offered both of those structures, as well as a standard cab, with either bench or bucket seating.

The new truck "is ahead of its class," Chevrolet said, focusing on the addition of side-curtain airbags, as well as General Motors' OnStar safety and security technology.

Compared to the S-10, the Colorado was built on a frame that was 250 percent stiffer. The midsize truck's stance was three inches wider. Even the standard cab was four inches longer.

The Colorado was built on wheelbases of 111.2 or 125.9 inches, three inches longer than the S-10 and a foot or more shorter than the Silverado.

For a while, the Isuzu i-Series truck was produced on the same assembly line as the Colorado, the similar GMC Canyon, and the Hummer H3.

The Colorado underwent a thorough updating for the 2007 model year. Changes included styling, features, and larger, more powerful inline engines.

However, it was not enough to turn the tide of customer demand. As the popularity of full-size trucks increased exponentially, demand for midsize trucks dwindled. In 2012, Chevrolet stopped producing the Colorado for US market.

A second-generation Colorado, exclusively

An S-10 gets a workout in off-road racing.

The latest generation of the Global S-10 was introduced in 2012.

for global markets, debuted at the 2011 Bangkok auto show in Thailand, which has become the second-largest pickup truck market in the world. General Motors opened a modern manufacturing facility in the country in 2000, producing right-hand-drive cars, sport utilities, and pickup trucks, including a version of the Colorado. These vehicles were also built in Egypt and South Africa in a joint venture with Isuzu.

A redesigned, larger US version of the second-generation Colorado followed as a 2015 model. It offered a 200-horsepower 2.5-liter four-cylinder and a 305-horsepower 3.6-liter V-6. For the 2016 model year—also a segment exclusive in the American midsize pickup market—Chevrolet offered a Duramax Diesel 2.8-liter four-cylinder turbodiesel engine with

369 pound-feet of torque and the capability of towing up to 7,700 pounds.

The new Colorado was built on wheelbases of 128.3 or 140.5 inches. The shorter platform was used for the extended cab model and offered a 6-foot, 2-inch pickup bed. The shorter platform also could be topped with a four-door crew cab with a 5-foot, 2-inch bed. The longer wheelbase was the basis for a crew cab verison with the longer pickup bed. Overall lengths were either 212.7 or 224.9 inches.

"The 2015 Colorado is tailored to the needs of customers in North America with distinctive design cues and a quiet, comfortable interior that offers car and crossover amenities," Marketing Director Sandor Piszar said as Chevrolet launched the truck. "It also offers innovative

ABOVE: The Colorado succeeded the S-10 in Chevrolet's US lineup.

LEFT: Chevrolet created this high-performance concept version of the Colorado in 2004.

Colorado extended cab.

features such as Chevy MyLink with a built-in available 4G LTE Wi-Fi hotspot, Lane Departure Warning and Forward Collision Alert."

Tailoring for the North American market meant the truck was built with extended and crew cabs only. Seats were designed for "long-haul comfort and wear," with dual firmness foam. In addition to advanced safety systems, Chevrolet MyLink and OnStar, and built-in Wi-Fi connectivity, it offered a GearOn system for cargo security.

"Meeting needs people didn't even know they have, that is what we saw as the opportunity for this truck," said Anita Burke, chief engineer for the new Colorado.

"When we looked at the segment, it was no wonder people weren't buying [midsize pickups]. They'd been very long neglected and were orphans and outdated and, frankly, pricey for what people got. People weren't buying them and why would they? With the Colorado, we saw an opportunity to attract buyers to Chevrolet as well as to the midsize segment itself."

So Burke and her team took a meaningful look at what the purpose should be for a midsize pickup.

"Midsize customers tend to drive their vehicles every day," she said, noting that they were used for commuting to work. The vehicles had to be functional for weekend recreation while also offering substantial capacity for work, and they needed to fit into parking structures and home garages equally well.

Burke went on:

Not everyone needs the full capability of a full-size truck. They don't need to tow horse trailers or have thousands of pounds of payload capability. But they still want a truck. They still want to tow. They still want to carry significant amounts of stuff. But they want it in a smaller package, the right size that meets their everyday needs.

And just because you want a box behind you, you shouldn't have to give up the creature comforts everyone's used to, a nice integrated interior, fabulous looking exterior. You shouldn't have to

A special off-road package and diesel engine completed the Colorado update for the 2017 model year.

BOTH: The latest version of the Chevrolet Colorado, introduced in 2015 and shown here in 2017 guise, was designed for people who don't need a full-size truck but who want or need to drive their pickup on a daily basis.

compromise, and that's why the segment wasn't doing well. The features weren't there. A lot of customers abandoned their wants of a pickup and went to a crossover because a full-size pickup was more than they needed. And they went away, sadly.

The Colorado was meant to change this situation, designed to meet customers' needs

before they realized they had them—and to put a smile back on their faces. The Colorado was incredibly successful—accounting for 25 percent of all midsize pickup sales in its first full year of production. In addition, Colorado won back-to-back Motor Trend's Truck of the Year awards in 2015 and 2016.

Suburban Living

Today, we recognize the Suburban as not only Chevrolet's oldest continually produced vehicle nameplate, but as the oldest such model designation within the entire American automobile industry. But just like the Chevrolet truck itself, the truck-based sport utility vehicle preceded its own official launch.

You may remember that two years before Chevrolet produced trucks for sale, its employees were turning Chevy 490 passenger cars into truck-style vehicles to move parts and supplies around within assembly plant complexes.

Chevrolet didn't officially launch its Carryall Suburban until the 1935 model year, but as early as 1926 you could buy a Chevrolet Superior half-ton Series V Springfield Suburban, a vehicle with three rows of seats covered by a wood-framed roof, the bodywork produced by automotive supplier Springfield Metal Body Company of Springfield, Massachusetts. Also available was Screenside Express, a similar vehicle but with screening instead of open expanses beneath the roof. In 1928, Chevrolet catalogs also listed the 1-ton Capitol Light Delivery Suburban model.

For the 1934 model year, Chevrolet restyled its half-ton trucks and in 1935 introduced the Carryall Suburban, an all-steel, eight-passenger station wagon, which was part of Chevrolet's upper-level Master series.

Significantly, this new Chevy was the first all-steel station wagon produced on a truck chassis. The Carryall Suburban was available in two-, three-, and four-door configurations, with a tailgate-style rear end for easy cargo access. Within a few years, side-hinged rear doors would become available.

Although today we fully associate the Suburban model with Chevrolet, that name had a much broader definition in the early days of the American auto industry. At that time, "Suburban" was a term applied to station wagon–style vehicles with windows along their sides—as opposed to the "sedan delivery" style which lacked side windows behind the front doors. Several automakers, including DeSoto, Studebaker, and Nash, produced Suburban models. After Plymouth discontinued its Suburban station wagon in 1978, General Motors gained full trademark rights to the name. Prior to that time, Chevrolet's Suburban officially bore "Carryall Suburban" nomenclature. Chevrolet and GMC both used Suburban badges on full-size

OPPOSITE: Far from the suburbs, a 1935 Chevrolet Suburban.

ABOVE: The 1935 Chevrolet Suburban featured three rows of seats beneath a wood-framed roof, and it still had room for camping and other gear.

RIGHT: A design sketch for the second-generation Chevrolet Suburban.

sport utility vehicles until 2000, when GMC rebranded its version as the Yukon XL.

Chevrolet's first Suburban was built on a 112-inch wheelbase, and was powered by the company's 206.8-cubic-inch straight six-cylinder engine, which was good for 60 horsepower, and was linked to a three-speed manual transmission. The engine was updated to provide 79 horsepower in 1936, 85 in 1938, and 90 in 1942. The wheelbase for Suburbans and other light half-ton trucks was stretched to 113.5 inches in 1939 and to 115 inches in 1941.

Like other Chevrolet trucks, Suburbans also got new front-end sheet metal and grille designs for the 1941 model year, which was considered the start of the Suburban's second generation. Production then shifted to military-use vehicles during World War II, including Carryall Suburbans, which were equipped to carry eight soldiers. Civilian production resumed for the 1946 model year, though it was based on pre-war designs with some engineering enhancements.

Chevrolet rolled out its Advance-Design generation of trucks for 1947 and the Suburban was among them. Though slightly larger in

TOP: Introduced for the 1941 model year, second-generation Suburbans had headlamps integrated into the front fenders, among other design updates.

ABOVE: An Omaha, Nebraska, Chevrolet dealership and its fleet of second-generation Suburbans.

displacement, the Thriftmaster Six engine was still rated at 90 horsepower. The next major change was another front-end redesign and the availability of a four-speed Hydra-Matic (automatic) transmission for the 1954 model year, when the six-cylinder engine's output exceeded the 100-horsepower plateau.

A next-generation Suburban was among the Task-Force trucks Chevrolet rolled out midway through the 1955 model year. Restyled and mechanically updated, the trucks were built on a 116-inch wheelbase and were available with Chevrolet's small-block V-8 engine tucked beneath their hoods. While the 235.5-cubic-inch six-cylinder was good for no more than 136 horsepower, the new 265-cubic-inch V-8 started at 154 horsepower and offered as much as 180 depending on the carburetor configuration. Two years later, the V-8 was enlarged to 283 cubic inches and as much as 270 horsepower.

Suburbans could also be equipped with factory-installed four-wheel drive, a feature that in ensuing years would become commonplace and help grow the

ALL: Design proposals for the post-war Advance-Design Suburban.

BOTH: Styling proposals for the Task-Force generation of Suburbans, introduced for the 1955 model year.

ABOVE: A designer's sketch for the 1960 Suburban with the "jet-pod" hood design . . .

RIGHT: . . . and the actual truck.

OPPOSITE BOTH: 1967 Chevrolet Suburbans are shown at play and at work.

sport utility vehicle category from niche to widespread popularity.

Not that anyone might have predicted as much when Chevrolet first rolled out its Carryall Suburban back in 1935. As Mike Mueller wrote in *Chevrolet Pickups*, "the rest of Detroit was slow to take notice." Except for the Suburban's GMC cousin, "no other knock-offs appeared in the 1930s. Although Willys-Overland did introduce a similar truck-based station wagon in 1946, it wasn't until International Harvester rolled out its attractive Travelall in 1956 that a true direct competitor emerged."

Suburbans and other Chevrolet trucks got new front-end treatments for 1958, the next-to-last year for the Task-Force generation. In

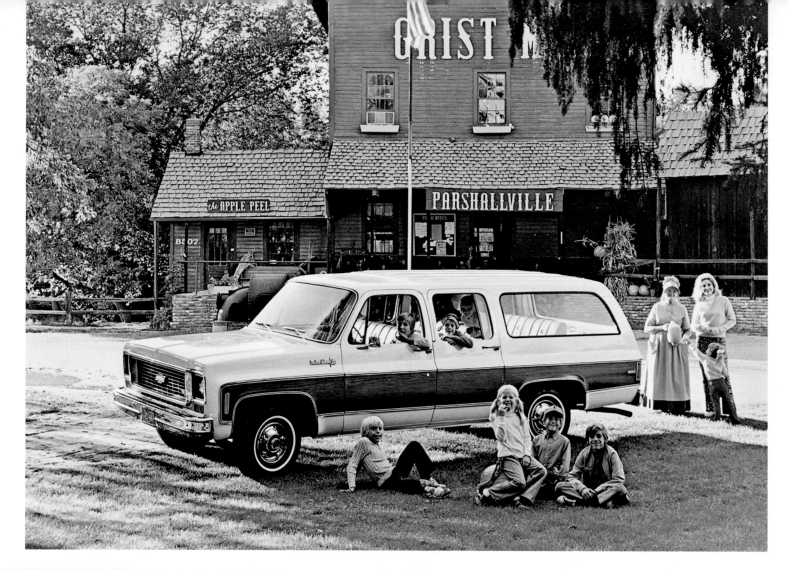

1960, Chevrolet introduced a new generation of trucks. The redesign featured "jet-pod" hoods and much more modern—longer and lower—styling, possible in part because of a redesign of the frames that underlay each truck. New independent front suspension led to a smoother, more comfortable ride.

In addition to design updates, larger and more powerful I6 and V-8 engines became available: In 1966, Suburban engine options included the 327-cubic-inch V-8 with 220 horsepower. A year later, Chevy trucks including the Suburban were redesigned and entered yet another generation, which ran through 1972.

In 1969, the Suburban gained a little brother as Chevrolet introduced the K5 Blazer, a sport utility built on a 104-inch wheelbase

BOTH: Suburban styling was updated in the mid-1970s.

BOTH: The Suburban underwent a major generational shift for the 1992 model year, changing not only its looks but increasing its towing capacity and interior space.

(the Suburban rode on a 127-inch base). The Blazer was produced with an open passenger compartment, though a removable hardtop was available for those who wanted protection from the elements. The Blazer eventually became available with rear- or four-wheel drive, but the four-wheel version was much more popular with consumers, who enjoyed exploring the true "sport" and "utility" nature of the vehicle.

For 1973, the Blazer's tailgate included a rear window that could be rolled up or down. In 1976, the Blazer got a steel "half-cab" body with a built-in roll bar and a roof that extended to just behind the front seats. The next year, Chevrolet offered customers an optional reinforced fiberglass rear roof section that attached to the main bodywork with sixteen bolts. The vehicle's popularity peaked in the late 1970s.

In 1992, the Blazer was moved to the then-new GMT400 chassis and came with a standard steel roof structure instead of the removable hardtop. The Tahoe, a full-size and truck-based sport utility much like the Suburban, replaced the Blazer in Chevrolet's SUV lineup in 1995. It was almost two feet shorter in overall length than the Suburban and rode on a wheelbase some fourteen inches shorter.

The Blazer name also was used on the smaller S-10 Blazer, which was based not on the full-size Chevrolet pickup truck but on the compact

OPPOSITE BOTH: The Country Coach was a special-edition Suburban produced for the 1973 through the 1980 model years. Known also as the Suburban Estate, it featured wood-grain exterior trim.

BELOW AND RIGHT: For the 1969 model year, Chevrolet introduced the K5 Blazer, a smaller-than-Suburban sport utility vehicle with a roofless passenger compartment.

ALL: For the 1973 model year, the Blazer had a tailgate with a built-in window that could be raised or lowered.

S-10. That vehicle would grow into the mid-sized TrailBlazer in the early years of the twenty-first century, until Chevrolet replaced its smaller and truck-based SUV with a group of car-based crossover utility vehicles.

Turning back to the Suburban, Chevy introduced an all-new version for 1973, with second- and third-row seating access improved by the addition of a road-side door behind the driver's. Those sitting in the second or third rows also benefitted from new air conditioning outlets. Chevrolet's big-block 454-cubic-inch V-8 engine was now available, though it initially

rated at only 240 horsepower (remember, this was the era of oil shortages and vehicle downsizing). Other advances during this generation were automatic locking front hubs on four-wheel drive Suburbans and the switch from carburetors to fuel injection.

The next-generation Suburban wasn't introduced until 1992. The Suburban celebrated its fifty-seventh year with a major facelift, a lowered step-in height, more room for people and cargo, and more towing capacity. The base engine was a 5.7-liter (350-cubic-inch) V-8 pumping out 190 horsepower with a

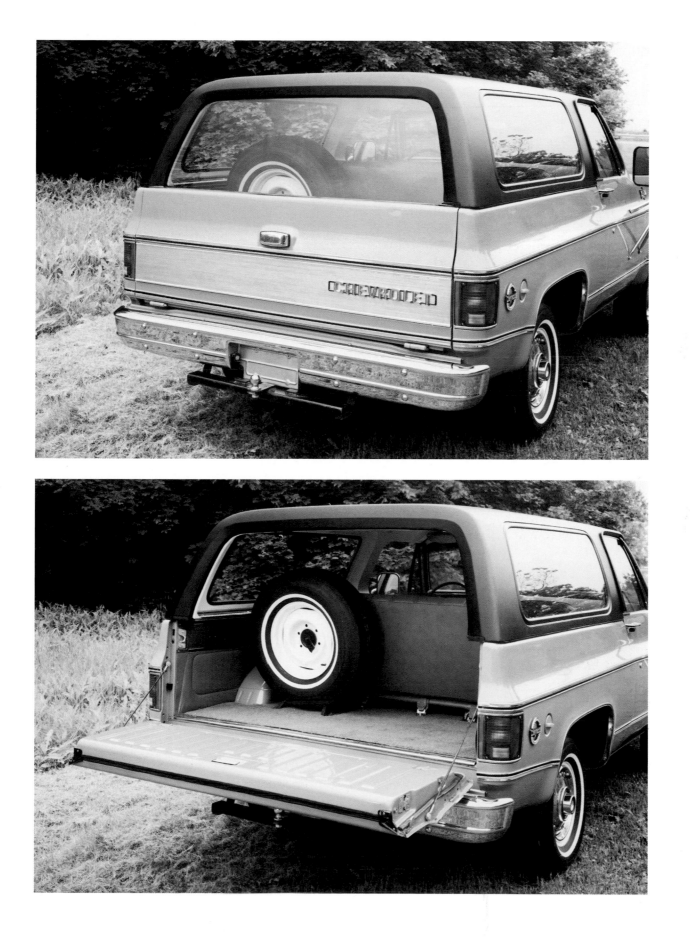

For 1977, the Blazer came with a "half-cab" steel body, and buyers could add an optional fiberglass rear roof section.

230-horsepower 7.4-liter with 385 pound-feet of torque on the options list for those who needed enhanced towing capacity.

And there were plenty of people who did. "Suburban" living didn't just mean living in the suburbs—ranchers with big trailers and people with mobile homes, boats, and other weekend toys all found the Suburban's improved towing capacity useful.

This was also the period when do-it-yourself home improvement was all the rage, and when big box stores were expanding and people needed vehicles that could bring home everything from 4x8 sheets of wallboard to big-screen televisions. The Suburban was more than capable in those regards, plus you could carry pretty much the entire youth soccer or hockey team in its three rows of seats.

Chevrolet introduced a next-generation Silverado pickup truck for 1999, and a next-gen Suburban followed for 2000. Initially, power came from new Vortec 5300 (5.3 liter) and 6000 (6.0-liter) V-8 engines, with larger and even more powerful engines soon to follow. The spare tire moved from inside the cargo area to beneath the SUV—a welcome change. This generation also got four-wheel disc brakes and was available with self-leveling suspension, with StabiliTrak vehicle dynamic control becoming standard during the 2005 model year. Upgraded interior accoutrements were added, as were such things as LTZ trim with 20-inch wheels.

For the 2007 model year, Chevrolet launched not only a new Silverado pickup truck, but the Avalanche and Suburban as well. Again, there were updates and improvements in seemingly

BOTH: By the early 1990s, the Chevrolet Blazer had moved from the compact S-10 platform to the half-ton pickup chassis, and was available in two- and four-door versions. In advertising, it was promoted as "a truck for wagon people."

RIGHT: Joining the Suburban in the full-size Chevrolet SUV lineup in the mid-1990s was the Tahoe, which was shorter in overall length.

BELOW: By the middle of the teen decade of the twenty-first century, the Chevrolet Suburban was a handsome sport utility with room inside for plenty of people and for all kinds of stuff, and with the towing capability to bring along even more on a trailer.

FOLLOWING PAGES: The 2017-model-year version of the Chevrolet Tahoe.

every system, from aerodynamics to interior, power to electronics, ride quality to vehicle safety systems.

A seventy-fifth anniversary edition of the Suburban with everything from navigation radio and rearview camera to heated and cooled front seats and 20-inch chrome wheels was offered during the 2010 model year. All 2,570 such units had LTZ trim and wore special white-diamond paint.

Suburban design was updated in 2015 with annual updates in features since, including rear-seat entertainment systems, low-speed forward automatic braking, Teen Driver features that allow parents to view an offspring's driving habits, and even 22-inch wheels, hands-free power lift gate, seating for nine, and much more.

Offering plenty of room inside for people and cargo, plenty of power for towing big loads, four-wheel drive for those times when the pavement ends, and with increasingly efficient powertrains, Suburban living has proven to be the lifestyle of choice, and not just for those living in the suburbs. From ranchers to recreational vehicle campers, the Suburban meets the needs of everyone.

CHEVY TRUCK LEGENDS: THE "BIG RED" SUBURBAN

Texas resident Chris DeMaio is launching a barbecue company and he's naming it Suburban Smoker after "Big Red," his 2003 Chevrolet Suburban.

"I was out of work," DeMaio said. "I needed something dependable to get to work [at his new job] and I couldn't afford repairs. I heard about a buddy who'd traded in a Suburban and I bought it. It had 130,000 miles on it."

Five years and nearly 75,000 miles later, all such issues are in the past.

"It's my everyday driver, whether pulling a trailer or going to work or packing everybody up and heading to the beach," he said. "It can do everything. I went to Lowe's recently and was putting twelve-foot-long fence beams into it and you can close the hatch on them—there's that much interior space, which is pretty awesome."

"I've owned a lot of cars—and some very expensive and exotic sports cars among them," he said. "But Big Red is definitely in the top three. I've fallen in love and I'll never get rid of it."

Fair and Square

In the 1950s, Dinah Shore sang about seeing the USA in your Chevrolet. But for the 1973 model year, and for more than a dozen years to follow, Chevrolet trucks were all about "building a better way to serve the USA." The 1973 sales brochure announced the new, so-called "square-bodied," Chevy pickup trucks noting that:

"We designed a completely new vehicle for '73 and tried to make it everything you've always wanted a truck to be. It's quiet and roomy inside. The ride is noticeably smoother. Glass area is large for improved visibility. Service is easy. And the new Chevy pickup looks like a light-duty truck ought to look."

That look was long and lean, chiseled and clean. Wherever possible, larger-section sheet metal panels were used to reduce joints and gaps. Another design innovation was squared rather than rounded wheelwells, a feature of Chevrolet trucks ever since.

"Most attractive was the Cheyenne model, which first appeared in 1971 to pick up where the CST [the 1967 Custom Sport Truck] left off and raise the luxury ante higher than ever," Mike Mueller writes in *Chevy Pickups.* "Along with two-tone paint and eye-catching exterior trim, the Cheyenne package also dressed up the Chevy truck interior to the nines."

Inside, the cabin not only was quieter but much more car-like and luxurious, with features such as tilt steering column, cruise control, updated audio, and even a rear window with a sliding center section that could open to enhance the new flow-through ventilation system. The dashboard was redesigned to put gauges and switchgear closer to the driver's eyes and hands.

The Cheyenne also offered vinyl bucket seats, deep-twist carpeting, a custom steering wheel, and special headliner and door trim.

A new four-door Crew Cab model also available in the now-iconic C30 one-ton Dooley, provided seating for as many as six people. Mueller notes that this new design was an immediate and huge hit with customers, many of them seemingly first-time pickup buyers:

"An even roomier cab went on top of a beefed-up frame, and exterior styling was jazzed up once more. More class, more luxury, and more options were among the goals that year. More and more sales resulted. In November 1973, Chevrolet announced that its half-ton Fleetside pickup had become General Motors' bestselling product, car or truck.

ABOVE: This 1976 Silverado Fleetside shows the square-body styling that was so popular with buyers then and still is with truck collectors today.

RIGHT: Cheyenne trim was the upscale version during the square-body era.

This achievement was partially credited to a new class of truck buyers—more prominently women and city folk—who had discovered that a hard-working pickup could also be an attractive second vehicle."

Hard-working, indeed. In addition to the design and luxury changes, the new C/K trucks could be equipped with a special camper package, new trailer-towing package, and even "Big Dooley" dual rear wheels beneath the Fleetside body style.

The 1973 C/K lineup offered buyers five engine choices, ranging from a 100-horsepower 250-cubic-inch V-6 to a 240 horsepower 454-cubic-inch big-block V-8, the latter providing 355 pound-feet of torque. In between were a 292 V-6 and 307- and 350-cubic-inch

V-8s. The 454 was being offered for the first time in a Chevrolet pickup with two-wheel drive (excluding the El Camino of the 1970s). Each of those engines could operate on no-lead, low-lead, or regular gasoline.

These trucks worked harder, they rode smoother. Wheelbases were extended by 2½ inches and strengthened. The rear suspension was redesigned with tapered, two-stage rear springs to enhance stability and load distribution. Rear axles were improved for enhanced durability. Rubber bushings helped cushion and quiet the ride as well. Front disc brakes were standard equipment. Two new four-wheel-drive models—K10 and K20—were added to the lineup. Pickup beds could have wood or steel floors to meet customer needs.

A Chevrolet pickup with Crew Cab architecture makes easy work of towing this big fifth-wheel travel trailer.

ABOVE: A 1974 Chevrolet C-10 Step Side delivers the news.

RIGHT: Chevy's 350 cubic-inch V-8 has the power to forge its own path as it takes this truck across the roadless Sonoran Desert.

To assure quality and durability, this new generation of Chevrolet trucks was years in the making, using extensive computer simulation even before prototypes were built and validated. Chevy's sales brochure stated: "We think we've accomplished what we set out to do: build the kind of truck you want. A truck that rides and handles better than any truck before. A truck that will give you the kind of gut feeling that it's the best-designed, best-built truck anywhere."

And that was saying something, because more than 58 percent of Chevrolet's 1957-model-year trucks were still on the road in 1973 and "no other make has even half [that percentage]. Evidence of how well Chevrolets are designed. How well they're built. And how well they serve the USA."

But that was just the starting point for this new generation of Chevrolet trucks.

For 1974, trucks were offered with full-time

(Continued on page 167)

Four-wheel drive enables Chevy trucks to deal with all sorts of road conditions, even when there are no roads to be found.

TOP: A ranch-ready Chevy truck; the step-in rear quarter-panel eased access to the truck bed.

ABOVE: This 1975 Scottsdale C20, equipped with Chevy's 350-cubic-inch V-8 engine, is ready for whatever work awaits it.

LEFT: A farm-fresh Chevy truck—and with those big mirrors, this one is all set for towing.

ABOVE: This Silverado has four doors and four rear wheels. Yes, it's a "Big Dooley."

RIGHT: Big Dooley can carry a load of lumber itself, plus even more on a trailer behind it.

OPPOSITE: A late '70s Chevy 4x4.

OPPOSITE TOP: A 1979 Silverado C10 in attractive two-tone colors.

OPPOSITE BOTTOM: The Crew Cab square-body had plenty of room for materials and for the people to use them at work.

ABOVE: Chevy trucks at work.

LEFT: Sometimes the reward for working hard was playing hard as well.

(Continued from page 159)

four-wheel drive, padded dashboards and the option of steel-belted radial tires. Grilles were restyled for 1975, and a Bonus Cab architecture (which we now call an Extended Cab) was available for that year for the C20, and soon was offered on an expanded list of models.

For 1977, there was a softer-suspension version of the four-wheel-drive K10, new steering wheel, and high-back bucket seats—but the big news that year was under the hood.

"As manufacturers were under pressure from the government and consumers to do more for less, the late '70s and '80s were fertile times for technological advancements," a Chevrolet news release reported. "Pure power, which was a luxury for passenger cars, was still a necessity for trucks in order to carry heavy loads. Chevrolet made a number of enhancements to its engines to help satisfy the need for outstanding power with enhanced fuel economy and improved emission levels. For example, diesel power was introduced to Chevy's light-duty truck line . . . to provide greater fuel economy, reduced fuel costs, and low emission levels."

The diesel, a V-8, had a displacement of 350 cubic inches and provided only 120 horsepower, but came through with 222 foot-pounds of torque.

A more aerodynamic hood was added for 1979. Radial tires became standard equipment on C and K models. Part-time four-wheel drive was new for 1980, as was an audio system with a cassette player. A new 6.2-liter diesel engine was an option for 1982. Grilles were redesigned again for 1983.

Automatic locking hubs were installed on 4x4 trucks for 1984, which meant drivers could switch from two- to four-wheel drive and back again without having to stop and manually unlock the front hubs. Then, just before the launch of the next-generation Chevrolet pickups, all gasoline-fueled engines were equipped with more efficient throttle-body fuel injection.

The square-body Chevy trucks remained in production for more than a dozen years. From 1955 to the point at which the last square-body rolled off an assembly line, Chevrolet had produced more than 18.5 million trucks and 11 million of them—nearly 60 percent!—were still on the road, working hard or ready for play.

1980 Chevrolet Silverado with diesel engine.

Muscular Trucks

On October 26–27, 1989, a Chevrolet pickup truck arrived at the Indianapolis Motor Speedway from the assembly line at Fort Wayne, Indiana. At the Speedway, the truck broke a 37-year-old production car record by averaging 103.463 miles per hour for 24 hours in laps around the 2.5-mile oval. Stopping only for fuel, tire, and driver changes, the truck, a C1500 Sport, traveled 993.234 laps, nearly 2,500 miles around the Brickyard, and was awarded the Hulman Indy Challenge Trophy.

The truck was driven by United States Auto Club racers Johnny Parsons, Rich Vogler, and Steve Butler. The C1500 Sport was powered by a 350-cubic-inch V-8 linked to a five-speed manual transmission; it was unmodified except for mandated safety equipment—a roll cage, five-point harness, fire extinguisher, extra instrumentation, and a tonneau cover over the truck bed. Additionally, the high-back driver's seat from a yet-to-be-released Chevrolet 454 SS pickup was installed, since it worked better with the safety harness system that secured the drivers.

The previous stock vehicle speed record at Indy was 89.93 miles per hour set by a Chrysler sedan in 1953. That a pickup truck became the new record holder said something about the place such vehicles held on American roads and in American driveways by the end of the 1980s.

The record-setting truck was a 1990 model, part of the "New Generation" of full-size pickup trucks that Chevrolet rolled out beginning with the 1988 model year. It was based on what was known internally as the GMT400 platform.

"We thought it was high time that somebody applied to the workhorse truck the same aerodynamics, electronics and materials technologies which have revolutionized the automobile in the past decade. So we did," said Robert Burger, then general manager of the Chevrolet division.

"The '88 Chevy full-size C/K pickup is state of the art," he added. "It's to full-size pickups what the pocket calculator was to the slide rule."

Even before its release for sale, it had established itself as the most dependable, longest-lasting truck on the road after traveling four million miles in development and validation engineering by GM staffers. In addition, early versions of the truck were loaned to farmers, contractors, and construction companies, which put another

OPPOSITE: A new generation of stronger, more powerful Chevrolet trucks rolls onto the roads.

2.9 million "real-world" miles on them to further validate the truck's readiness for long-term duty.

Burger explained that customers buy pickup trucks for two primary reasons: durability and longevity. He said the new Chevrolet offered those, plus uncompromising user-comfort features.

To get that message across—and to help convince truck buyers of the durability and dependability of its newest pickup truck—Chevrolet once again launched an advertising campaign with a theme song that symbolized the company and its vehicles. The song, "Like a Rock," by Detroit's very own Bob Seger, took its place as a quintessential American anthem. In 2006, the twenty-fifth anniversary of the release of the iconic album featuring the song, *Rolling Stone* reported:

Chevrolet claimed to have the longest lasting and most dependable pickup trucks on the market and needed something that really drove that home. Toyota, Subaru and other foreign carmakers were selling more cars during the recession America found itself in at the start of the decade, but light truck sales (vans, SUVs and pickups) by American auto companies were still strong. Chevy, which had always found new ways of tying patriotic duty with buying cars, from the Eisenhower-era "See the USA in Your Chevrolet" to 1970s and 1980s campaigns like "Baseball, Hotdogs, Apple Pie & Chevrolet" and "The Heartbeat of America," really needed something that hit home what made their pickups better than all others.

OPPOSITE TOP: Scottsdale was one of the Chevrolet C/K full-size pickup trim packages.

ABOVE AND OPPOSITE BOTTOM: Silverado was the top-of-the-line version of the full-size Chevrolet pickup truck.

It's Got A Mean Streak.

- 7.4-liter, fuel-injected V8 engine.
- 405 lbs.-ft. of torque. 255 horsepower.
- 4-speed electronic-shift automatic transmission.
- Dual exhaust.

Chevy 454 SS. Now with even more horsepower and torque. The world's most powerful production ½-ton pickup just got meaner. The Chevy 454 SS. It's so serious it only comes in black. And it's another reason more truck owners switched to Chevy last year than to any other truck.*

More People Are Winning With *The Heartbeat* of America. TODAY'S TRUCK IS CHEVROLET.

Some might consider the 454 SS to be a monster truck, what with a 7.4-liter V-8 beneath its hood.

On paper, there is something perfect about a Detroit automaker using a song by a hometown guy like Seger for one of their commercials . . . [For Seger] there was something about working with the auto manufacturer that felt right. "I'm a Michigan guy," he told the *Detroit Free Press* in 1994. "My father worked at Ford for 19 years, I worked at GM in Ypsilanti . . ."

The song just embodied everything Chevy wanted to say about what was great about their trucks: that they'd still be there standing straight and bold after a day of hard work, that they'd be "carryin' the weight," that they were solid and tough to break—like a rock . . .

The initial commercial set the template for the campaign that would last until 2004: plenty of mud-covered pickups, cattle, cowboys, people in hard hats and American flags all set to Seger.

With its new truck, Chevrolet offered those farmers, hard-hat-wearing workers, and all-American pickup buyers a "New Generation" vehicle that was durable and dependable, while also offering an extended-cab architecture with seating for three in the back row. And, although the new truck's aerodynamic design made it narrower than its predecessor model, the cabin actually was wider on the inside. Doors were larger and step-in height was lower, making egress easier. As with previous truck generations, Chevrolet made its new trucks more functional and more comfortable for customers to use. The larger cabin was further enhanced by having a third more glass area.

Only the engines—a V-6 and three V-8s—and the trim names—Cheyenne, Scottsdale, and Silverado—were carried over from the previous generation of trucks. While those names continued, the former Stepside exterior sheet metal was now termed Sportside, featuring steps in front of and behind the rear wheel to ease reaching into the truck bed.

New for 1990 were a no-frills Work Truck version and the previously mentioned limited-production, high-performance 454 SS: a pickup truck with performance car chops.

Changes for 1991 primarily involved technology enhancements for engines and

transmissions and some updates to audio and air conditioning systems.

The big news for 1992 was a four-door crew cab passenger compartment for one-ton pickups. This architecture wouldn't be available on the half-ton trucks until the end of the decade, when the next generation was introduced.

Engines were updated for 1993 and again for 1996, when Chevrolet pickup truck sales reached nearly 1.5 million units.

Extended cab pickups got a third door (on the passenger side) to enhance access to the back seating area in 1997. There were no major changes for 1998 because yet another all-new and next-generation pickup was in the pipeline for 1999.

Chevrolet was quite proud of the powertrain that propelled its 454 SS muscle truck.

The beauty of a sport truck. The subtlety of a sledgehammer.

7.4 Liter V8 engine.   Sport suspension with gas shocks.   B.F. Goodrich Comp T/A high-performance radials.   3-year/50,000-mile Bumper to Bumper Plus Warranty.*

To The Sharper Image the idea was more than just a little intriguing. A production pickup with more raw horsepower than some of the world's best-known sport cars.

Think of it. A two-seater with 7.4 liters of fuel-injected V8 muscle under the hood. That can pull more than .8 g's in a corner.† That can go from 0-50 in just 6.30 seconds.† It's the Chevy 454 SS. The world's most powerful production ½-ton pickup.

If products with imagination are what catch the eye of The Sharper Image, it's safe to say they couldn't take their eyes off the new Chevy 454 SS. Its power and personality are what helped make Chevy Truck the Official Vehicle of The Sharper Image. Nobody's winning like The Heartbeat of America.

THE *Heartbeat* OF AMERICA IS WINNING   TODAY'S TRUCK IS CHEVROLET™

*See your Chevrolet dealer for terms of this limited warranty. A deductible applies after 12 months or 12,000 miles. †On a test track with a professional driver. Chevrolet and the Chevrolet emblem are registered trademarks and Chevy is a trademark of the GM Corp. ©1989 GM Corp. All Rights Reserved. Let's get it together...buckle up.

454 SS

The late 1960s and early 1970s were the heyday for Detroit muscle cars, vehicles such as the Chevrolet Impala 409, Chevrolet Chevelle SS396, and Chevrolet Camaro Z/28. But pickup truck owners didn't get a chance to partake in the high-horsepower fun (unless they opted for performance versions of the El Camino).

That changed with the 1990 model year, when Chevrolet launched the 454 SS, a very special version of its half-ton Fleetside pickup truck.

Based on the latest generation of the full-size C/K introduced in 1988, the 454 SS was built in the same spirit that propelled the historic Detroit muscle cars—finding a way to cram the largest engine possible into the space beneath the hood. Now, however, new developments in technology made it possible to offer a complete dynamic package.

"It's a one-of-a-kind C1500 Regular-Cab Short-Box with the largest V-8 in a regular-production half-ton pickup today," a Chevrolet sales brochure boasted.

That V-8 was a L19 7.4-liter (454 cubic-inch) powerplant pumping out 230 horsepower and 385 pound-feet of torque.

The engine was linked to a three-speed automatic transmission. Also included were a locking rear differential with 3.73 axle ratio and a unique rear axle, a ZQ8

performance suspension that featured Bilstein gas shock absorbers, engine oil cooler, heavy-duty radiator, and transmission oil cooler.

The truck was available only in ominous Onyx Black paint with tinted glass, halogen-composite headlamps, special low-profile blackwall tires, and a Garnet Red cloth interior with high-back Sport bucket seats, center console, Comfortilt Sport steering wheel, AM/FM/cassette audio system, air conditioning, sliding rear windows, power locks and windows, auxiliary lighting, and intermittent wipers.

The 454 SS truck got a power boost for the 1991 model year, with horsepower rising to 255 and torque to 405 foot-pounds. The rear axle was changed to a 4:10:1 ratio for better off-the-line acceleration, a dual exhaust system was installed, and a four-speed automatic transmission was available.

The 454 SS was also available for the 1992 and 1993 model years, with Summit White and Victory Red exterior colors and additional interior colors.

The 454 SS was a truck designed to be fast, and it carried an RPO code worthy of a personalized license: B4U. Indeed.

ABOVE: At introduction, the Chevrolet 454 SS pickup truck was available only in sinister Onyx Black paint with tinted windows.

The 454 SS had a red cloth interior with high-back bucket seats and other special features.

Silverado Emerges

"How do you improve the most dependable, longest-lasting full-size pickup?" Chevrolet asked. Its 1999 truck brochure provided the answer:

You make it bigger, faster, stronger, and smarter. You build the all-new Silverado from Chevrolet.

A truck has a job to do, and our full-size C/K Pickup did it about as well as could be done. But we knew we could build a better truck. And we did.

Replacing a legend is never easy. So we built a new benchmark. The 1999 Silverado. The Truck. From Chevrolet. Like A Rock.

Turn the page in that brochure and the headline reads: "Generations of Tradition." What the printing trade calls a "double-truck" photograph showed the last six generations of Chevrolet trucks, parked side by side. Standing next to the new Silverado were two baseball legends: Cal Ripken, Senior and Junior.

"It's all about heritage," the copy stated.

For more than 80 years, Chevrolet has been building trucks that Americans have counted on. When you've been upholding that responsibility for as long as we have, you tend to know a lot about your product ... and what your customers expect. That's why we say Silverado is literally everything we've learned and everything we know about building pickups. Like the name "Ripken" on the back of a baseball jersey, the gold bowtie you'll find on every Silverado means something special. That is, when there's a job to do—when there are people depending on you—we'll be there day after day, generation after generation. That's our heritage. Chevy Trucks—still the most dependable, longest-lasting trucks on the road.

Talk about longest lasting: Cal Ripken Sr. had been a player, scout, coach, or manager with the Baltimore Orioles baseball team for thirty-six years. Talk about most dependable: Ripken's son played for the team for twenty-one years and broke a fifty-six-year-old major league record established by Lou Gehrig of the New York Yankees: Ripken Jr. didn't miss a day of work for more than a decade as he played in a record 2,632 consecutive games. Could there be two more emblematic men to represent Chevy's new truck?

OPPOSITE: Even in its most basic form, a Chevrolet Silverado is designed to meet its owner's needs, be they in a farm field, a construction site, or a suburban shopping center.

Chevrolet was so happy to offer a new truck with so many features that it renamed its full-size pickup model the Silverado, previously the top-of-the-line trim package.

Turn another page in that 1999 Chevrolet brochure and there's another double-truck image, an overhead view of the plush, five-seat interior of the new Chevrolet Silverado extended cab, although it looks as if we're viewing the interior of some large, leather-bound luxury sedan. The cabin was the largest available in any half-ton pickup, a full four inches longer than the previous Chevrolet C/K offered. It offered the widest rear seat in a pickup on the market, enhanced front-seat travel, the most legroom, the widest third-door opening, more storage, and overachieving comfort.

Turn the page again and see "the most powerful V-8 engine of any pickup truck." The new Vortec 4800, 5300, and 6000 V-8s had been built for the new Silverado, and each had more power and a longer, flatter torque curve than previous engine options. Horsepower ratings were 255, 270, and 300, respectively, with torque figures of 285, 315, and 355. And there was a Vortec 4300 V-6 as well, with 200 horsepower and 280

BOTH: A rear-hinged door provides access to the extended-cab's rear seat.

pound-feet of torque. A 6.5-liter turbo diesel engine also was available.

The brochure also highlighted the new Silverado's dashboard—"Silverado, it's smarter"—with features such as push-button-activated four-wheel drive, seven-pin plug-in trailer connections, even a driver message center to let you know when it's time for an oil change.

An all-new frame underpinned the new Silverado as well. It was the first three-piece modular frame for a light-duty pickup and was strengthened with features such as tubular cross members and a state-of-the-art, hydroformed front section (made from a piece of steel tubing shaped under water pressure and thus without joints or welds, a process that had debuted a couple of years earlier on the Chevrolet Corvette).

As the brochure noted, "You can't have the most dependable, longest-lasting truck without a solid foundation."

The brochure wrapped up with a tidy summary of the Silverado's multiple missions. "Strong enough for dirty work," we read over a photo of the new Silverado plowing through the mud. "Comfortable enough for office work" is the headline over yet another interior view. "Roomy enough for homework," it says over a photograph of a dad and his children. "Forget the limo. Take the truck" appears above a photograph of a bride and groom getting ready to drive away from their wedding in a new Silverado. Missions accomplished.

For several years, Silverado had been the name applied to the top-of-the-line version of the Chevrolet C/K pickup truck line. "With all of the value, technology and new features packed into this truck, it deserves the Silverado name," Silverado brand manager Kurt Ritter said when the new naming format was revealed. Instead of place names, the trim levels were base, LS and LT, as with other Chevrolet vehicles.

The new Silverado won truck-of-the-year honors from *Motor Trend* and, two years later, the new heavy-duty version of the Silverado took the same accolades from the magazine.

In between, Chevrolet "pushed the envelope" when it unveiled a radical pickup truck concept vehicle at the 2000 North American International Auto Show in downtown Detroit. The concept was called the Chevrolet Avalanche.

Part pickup truck, part sport utility vehicle, the Avalanche was built on a truck chassis, but it had a cabin much like that found in the Chevrolet Suburban. However, instead of a

BOTH: 2500 badging
indicates this as a
heavy-duty pickup.

third-row seat, the Avalanche had a pickup-style "cargo box."

A "midgate" behind the second-row seats could be opened, the rear backlight removed and stowed, and those seats folded to provide for an extended pickup bed.

The versatile and innovative Avalanche went from concept to production vehicle for the 2002 model year and immediately won *Motor Trend*'s SUV-of-the-year honors. It also provided the basis for the upscale Cadillac Escalade EXT. With as much as 12,000 pounds of towing capacity, a choice of two V-8 engines and four-wheel-drive capability, it also became popular with recreational truck users. Sales topped fifty thousand units for each of the first seven years of production, peaking at more than ninety-four thousand in 2003.

Meanwhile, a four-wheel steering system, Quadrasteer, was introduced on the Silverado for the 2003 model year. The system was designed to ease low-speed maneuvers, including parking, while also enhancing high-speed stability.

A Crew Cab with four full-size doors joined the Silverado lineup for the 2004 model year.

Engines and entertainment systems were also upgraded, and 2003 saw the new Silverado SS, a high-performance pickup with a 345-horsepower, 6.0-liter V-8, Hydra-matic transmission, all-wheel drive, and 20-inch wheels with Goodyear Eagle tires.

A crew cab with four full doors joined the Silverado lineup for 2004. A year later, extended and crew cabs could be equipped with power sun roofs. And, for the 2007 model year, yet another new generation of full-size Chevrolet pickups was ready to roll onto roads and work sites. The next generation of Silverado pickups would bring sophisticated new technologies along with even more capability to meet the needs of Chevrolet customers.

ABOVE: For years, sport utility vehicles had been built atop pickup truck chassis. Chevrolet reversed the process to produce the Avalanche, a pickup truck based on the Suburban SUV, but with a pickup truck bed in the back.

RIGHT: With four-wheel drive, Avalanche was sure-footed in the snow.

CHEVY TRUCK LEGENDS: LONZO ANDERSON

Police officer Lonzo Anderson's shift ended at 7:00 a.m. one morning and he was on his way home when his car caught fire. "I was totally embarrassed," Anderson admitted, to be a first-responder who needed first responders to help with the situation.

Fortunately for Anderson, just across the road from his burning car was Ray Vandergriff's Arlington, Texas, Chevrolet dealership.

"I needed a vehicle to get to work that night," Anderson recalled. So, he bought a new 2000 Chevrolet Silverado 1500 with blue paint, a 5.3-liter V-8 under its hood, and "4 miles on the odometer," he said.

A decade and a half later, that odometer displays some 375,000 miles.

Anderson's goal is to reach half a million miles, retire the truck, and buy another. A Chevy, of course.

Building on Silverado's Heritage

As one General Motors executive explained it, power, pulling, and payload used to define the full-size pickup truck segment. By 2006, though, those attributes merely represented the price of entry into the marketplace. To make the move from showroom curiosity to truck worthy of purchase, people demanded more from their trucks: more style, more features, more room, more comfort, more convenience, more refinement, more towing capacity, more cargo capability, more safety and security. And don't overlook more fuel efficiency.

Such were the goals when Chevrolet rolled out the next-generation Silverado pickup trucks (and a new Avalanche) for the 2007 model year. The new truck, Chevrolet said, was rooted in having been "on the job, day in and day out, generation after generation," for going on ninety years. Improved in six key product areas, this new Silverado was "the culmination of nearly a century of genuine, real-world testing."

Based on the new GM900 truck platform, this newest-generation Silverado—both light- and heavy-duty models—featured improvements in design and aerodynamics, interior accoutrements, ride and handling, power, safety, and even warranty, with a 100,000-mile/five-year powertrain program. Trucks were available in regular, extended, and crew-cab architecture; with two- and four-wheel drive; with short (5-foot, 8-inch), standard (6-foot, 6-inch), and long (8-foot) beds; and in WT, LT, and LTZ trim as well as an LS exterior styling option.

Speaking of the new truck's design, Chevrolet offered a broad, chiseled face with a wider, taller grille and power-dome hood; a powerful, muscular yet lower stance; a windshield slanted back at 57 wind-cheating degrees; jeweled stacked headlights; door handles designed for those wearing work gloves; and extended cab rear access doors that opened 170 degrees. In addition, it featured a step built into the corners of the rear bumper to ease the effort to climb or to reach into the truck bed.

The new trucks offered perhaps the most remarkable option ever in any vehicle interior: the customer could choose between two different interior designs. One was "pure pickup," while the other was more like that found in a luxury car or sport utility. Each offered its own seats, instrument and door panels, consoles, glove box (or boxes), storage solutions, switch-gear, trim, and other features.

In either case, the instrument panel was lower and farther forward than in any previous Chevrolet truck.

OPPOSITE: "Farm fresh" is an adjective that means something to fine cooks. But it also can apply to a truck that is ready for whatever chores it faces—on the farm or the work site or on a night on the town.

ABOVE: Chevrolet introduced the second generation of its Silverado full-size pickup family for the 2007 model year. The trucks (a 2007 Chevrolet Silverado LT Z71 Crew Cab is shown) were redesigned inside and out, and were packed with updated technological features.

RIGHT: Texans buy more full-size pickup trucks than the residents of any other state.

MEXICO'S CHEVROLET TRUCK BRIGADE

This amazing and inspiring story comes from Jorge Covarrubias and the Cheyenne Brigade Mexico:

We have been traveling for more than six years, providing relief help in remote areas of Mexico with our Chevrolet Cheyenne pickup trucks. Each trip is an adventure.

For example, on one trip we carried a large cargo of drinking water to a storm-ravaged city. In another location, a river had raged out of control, carrying with it a house occupied by elderly people. Another time, a man of fierce appearance, with a single eye and a wooden leg, came to us with a loud voice to thank us for the materials we'd just delivered.

We have carried chickens to those who needed them, transported lights so children could see to do their homework, and driven up mountains so high that airplanes were flying below us.

So far, we have traveled more than 400,000 kilometers (nearly 250,000 miles) and more than 500,000 people have benefited from the Chevrolet Brigade and their ability to carry whatever is needed to wherever it is needed. And one of the most important things we carry is hope.

Silverado models were more spacious inside, with increased storage capacity. Spaciousness was enhanced with new, "low and forward" instrument panels. The instrument panel offered as part of the LTZ trim level was 5 inches lower and farther forward than the previous model. The WT and LT trim level featured an instrument panel 3½ inches lower and further forward.

Second-row seats in extended and crew cabs were more supportive and had new, more comfortable seat-back angles. Extended cabs had more legroom and power windows that lowered all the way to the sills. Crew cabs had elevated rear seats for better visibility.

Even DVD entertainment systems were available, as were touchscreen navigation and other features.

Truck beds could be equipped with a built-in cargo management system. The sales brochure included towing information and pointed out that a Silverado "always pulls its own weight. And up to five tons more." Tow/haul technology adjusted transmission shift points and reduced throttle pedal motion to make towing smoother.

Ride and handling benefited from a fully boxed frame, new coil-over front suspension, rack-and-pinion steering, wider front and rear tracks, and five different suspension setups, each tailored to specific driving needs, from towing to off-road travel to enhanced performance on the street. The trucks also had a new anti-lock braking system; StabiliTrak, GM's electronic stability control, was standard on all crew cab models and new to the full-size truck segment.

Seven gasoline or flex-fuel engines were available, providing more power but also enhanced fuel economy. They ranged from a 4.3-liter V-6 to a 6.0-liter V-8 rated at 367 horsepower.

In addition to StabiliTrak (which became standard on all Silverados with the 2010 model year), trucks featured a suite of safety and convenience items, including a full array of airbags, OnStar Safe & Sound, and tire-pressure monitors, and could be equipped with remote starters and rear parking assist technology.

But Chevrolet didn't stop there in making its Silverado the most flexible vehicle possible for its customers. Soon, satellite radio was added to the list of standard features, and a hybrid-powered Silverado gas/electric version offered 25 percent more fuel-efficiency. Other additions included a six-speed automatic transmission and rearview camera, heated and cooled front seats, and StabiliTrak updated with electronic trailer sway control and hill-start assist technology.

For the 2014 model year, Chevrolet pickups were built on an updated platform known within Chevrolet as the "K2." And while the trucks were new "from hood to hitch," as Chevrolet put it, with three new engines, with a quieter cab

OPPOSITE BOTH: High Country Silverado is more than capable of hauling a livestock trailer.

BELOW: Chevy's Silverado is at home in the city as much as on the ranch or farm.

with more features, with updated technologies to improve ride and handling, and with cargo management systems for the bed, there was no change in the Silverado's base pricing. The trucks also came with 24,000 miles or two years of maintenance included in that price.

"When you combine the innovative features of the new Silverado with comparable pricing to 2013 models and standard scheduled maintenance, Silverado becomes a great choice for pickup customers, helping them save money when they buy—and when they drive," said Jeff Luke, the Silverado's global chief engineer.

The new engines, a V-6 and two V-8s, were more powerful but also more fuel efficient, Chevrolet noted, "without the cost and complexity of turbocharging." The engines provided enhanced towing capacity. For the 2014 model year, the 6.2-liter V-8 provided 420 horsepower and 460 pound-feet of torque and best-in-class towing capacity of 12,500 pounds. Chevrolet's Silverado 1500 lineup had the best-in-class V-8 towing and fuel efficiency.

An updated design contributed to fuel economy. The styling included rear doors on

(Continued on page 198)

ABOVE: Z71 is the special off-road package for the Chevrolet Silverado.

OPPOSITE: Chevrolet has given a new status to the term "farm truck."

FOLLOWING PAGES: A High Country special-edition Silverado dualie looks right at home on the ranch.

Special-edition pickups have become very popular with customers. This is the 2016 Silverado 2500 HD Z71 Midnight Edition, offering off-road equipment combined with a monochromatic black appearance.

(Continued from page 195)
crew-cab models that were larger for easier access to the back seat. Rear doors on double-cab models were hinged in front rather than at the rear for easier access, especially in tight quarters, such as parking lots.

Crew cab trucks now were offered with a longer 6-foot, 6-inch pickup box, providing more cargo capacity while still fitting into many home garages.

Another new feature was Chevrolet's MyLink, providing available Wi-Fi, and with voice recognition technology.

New for 2015 was the Silverado High Country version, which Chevrolet said "embodies rugged luxury—craftsmanship,

authenticity and functionality rolled into a truck that's stronger, smarter and more capable than ever. It is Chevrolet's first premium truck." In addition to special exterior appointments, including 20-inch chrome wheels, the High Country got a saddle-brown interior with heated and cooled front leather bucket seats.

Next came the new features, such as a remote-locking tailgate, eight-speed automatic transmission, Apple CarPlay and Android Auto capability, lane-keeping assist technology, a factory spray-in bedliner, new front-end styling, 12,500-pound towing capacity for crew cab models, low-speed forward automatic braking technology, and a new 6.6-liter Duramax diesel engine that provided the Silverado HD with 445 horsepower and a whopping 910 pound-feet of torque.

Capping all this progress was the culmination of the latest Silverado generation: a Centennial edition for the 2018 model year.

"One hundred years of Chevy trucks, a centennial event, is very important, certainly in the life of a person it's a very rare thing," said Luke. "One hundred years is a long time for any entity or any activity."

Luke, who bought his first C/K when he was a college student in 1985 and has been part of the GM truck team since not long after earning his engineering degree a year later, noted that Chevrolet trucks have evolved throughout their history:

from very early vehicles that largely were intended to move stuff and a passenger to where they are today, where they are an alternative to a luxury vehicle that provides a tremendous amount of versatility and for hauling stuff and for towing. It's everything from work to play, and with high levels of safety, quiet, fuel economy. They are designed and executed to meet the needs of the most demanding customers, and customers need to know that we're designing to their needs.

There are no gimmicks on our Chevrolet trucks. They're practical. They're tried and true.

For the 2017 model year, Chevrolet introduced a heavy-duty Silverado. It was powered by a new Duramax Diesel engine that provides a stunning 910 pound-feet of torque.

The Centennial Truck and Beyond

"Hi, guys," the host says, "today we're here to talk about the Chevy Silverado special edition..." Thus begins a television commercial, launched in late December 2016, to introduce not just a special edition of the Chevrolet Silverado pickup truck—a monochrome white vehicle that looks dazzling parked in a dark, hangar-style building—but five different special-edition trucks, the others suddenly and dramatically emerging from various hiding places, including one lifted by elevator from beneath the building's floor.

Since that commercial was shot, two more special-edition Silverados have been created, and perhaps the most special of all will be unveiled as part of the Chevrolet Truck Centennial celebration.

The white truck at the center of the commercial is the Custom Sport special edition, available on 2500 Crew Cab LT and LTZ models, riding on 20-inch polished aluminum wheels, with a body-color grille and bumpers; chrome door handles, mirror caps, and bodyside molding; and with a spray-in bedliner and front- and rear-park assist technology.

Other special-edition Silverados include:

Alaskan: A Chevrolet Silverado designed for winter weather. Built on the Silverado 2500HD, the Alaskan edition rides on 18-inch black aluminum wheels with Goodyear Wrangler tires to take full advantage of the 6.0-liter Vortec or available 6.6-liter Duramax Turbo-Diesel V-8 engine. The trucks feature Alaskan Bear graphics, smoked amber roof marker lights and beacon, a spray-in bedliner with the Bowtie logo, and a special snow plow prep package.

Black Out: A model 1500 regular or double cab work truck (WT) with black 20-inch wheels, black Bowtie emblems, a black grille and headlamp bezels, and deep-tinted windows.

High Desert: A special edition for the LT, LTZ, and High Country Silverados, the High Desert has a sport bar with sail panel at the front of the bed, and a flexible and lockable storage system in the bed that includes lighted side-storage boxes beneath a hard-folding tonneau cover. LTZ High Country models ride on 20-inch wheels, and can be equipped with an EcoTec3 6.2-liter V-8 engine and High Country standard ride control.

Midnight: Available on Silverado crew and double cab trucks and Silverado HD trucks with the Z71 package. Colorado Midnight rides on black 18-inch wheels with Goodyear Duratrac

OPPOSITE: The Centennial special edition of the Chevrolet Silverado displays its heritage in many ways, including a retro-styled bowtie badge on its grille.

BOTH: Midnight HD is one of the special-edition Chevrolet Silverados and Colorados available for the 2017 model year.

PREVIOUS PAGES: The Colorado (left) and Silverado (right) Redline edition.

off-road tires, has black bumpers and grill, black Bowtie emblems, larger Z71 badges, and spray-in bedliners with Bowtie logo.

Rally 1 and Rally 2: These special editions of the Silverado 1500 come in Black, Summit White, Red Hot, or Silver Ice Metallic colors with rally stripes and black Bowtie emblems. Rally 1 trucks ride on 20-inch black wheels; the Rally 2s are 22 inches.

Realtree: The Silverado is designed for outdoor enthusiasts and starts with a black 1500 Crew Cab LTZ or Z71 truck that gets special exterior camouflage graphics from Realtree—

the outdoor equipment and clothing manufacturer—plus embroidered headrests with camouflage accents, a black leather interior, blacked-out bowtie emblems, black off-road assist steps, larger Z71 badging, and spray-in bedliners with a Realtree graphic. These trucks ride on Rancho shocks for enhanced off-pavement performance.

Redline: A full-size pickup with an urban-inspired design featuring red and black accents. Available on LT Z71 double cabs and LTZ Z71 crew cabs, Redline features include 20-inch black wheels with red accents, black

Silverado badges with a red outline, red tow hooks, off-road assist steps, black bowties, mirror caps, grille and headline trim, body-color front and rear bumpers, and a spray-in bedliner with Bowtie logo.

Special Ops: Another special-edition partnership truck from Chevrolet, this time with the Navy SEAL Museum in Fort Pierce, Florida. This edition's mission is to help the families of fallen, injured, and active-duty military personnel through the Trident House Charities Program. These Silverado 1500 WT double cabs have special Navy-inspired blackout graphics, black aluminum wheels, deep-tinted windows, black bowties, a bed-mounted sport bar with the Special Ops signature, sport-assist steps, all-terrain tires, and spray-in bedliner with Bowtie logo.

And it's not just the Silverado that comes in special-edition versions. There are Redline, Custom, and Midnight versions of the Chevrolet Colorado midsize truck, as well as a Shoreline special edition that can be equipped with GearOn tiered storage racks, a Thule stand-up paddle board carrier, and rectangular rear-assist steps to ease access to such equipment in the truck bed.

"The bandwidth is extremely broad," Jeff Luke, Global Chief Engineer for Chevrolet Trucks, said of the Silverado special edition program. And, he added, such trucks tend to sell quickly.

There's also a Texas Silverado edition featuring special badging that's become so popular with customers that it's now available at dealerships outside the Lone Star State.

"[Special edition] buyers tend to be our most enthusiastic fans," said Sandor Piszar, Marketing Director at Chevrolet Trucks.

Which brings us to perhaps the most special of these special-edition trucks: the Centennial Special Edition Silverado 1500 and Colorado.

"With the upcoming centennial of Chevrolet trucks, our loyal customers told us this is a milestone they want to celebrate," Piszar said.

"A centennial event is a very important event," Luke said. "One hundred years is a very long time for a person, an entity, or an activity. Even before we went prime time one hundred years ago, there was a one-ton [truck] and we had vehicles that were moving stuff around at our plant, and in some cases [trucks] were being sent overseas as ambulances and other vehicles for World War I."

Luke said it's instructive to see how trucks have evolved "from very early vehicles that largely were intended to move stuff and a driver to where they are today, where they are an alternative to a luxury car that provides a tremendous amount of versatility, including hauling and towing stuff. It's everything from work to play, and with high levels of safety, quiet, and fuel economy.

"They've gone from a flat bed to a wood bed to [today's] high-strength, roll-formed steel bed purposely designed and executed to meet the needs of the most demanding customers," Luke said.

Chevrolet's proud history will be celebrated in the Centennial-edition trucks, which will wear Blue Steel Metallic exterior paint with 22-inch wheels, chrome accents, and exclusive Heritage Bowtie badging.

The blue color selected pays homage to the 1918 Series D and 1926 Superior Series V trucks, as well as to the 1936 Suburban and Canopy Express.

A Chevrolet Silverado can take on an almost mysterious appearance when equipped with the Midnight special-edition package.

The bowtie badges on the 1918 and 1926 vehicles were chrome plated and filled with blue enamel paint, or were made from chromed cloisonné with a blue enamel background and white enamel lettering. On the Centennial trucks, the chrome surrounds will be the same shape as the modern gold bowtie emblem with the center finished in dark blue. The chrome lettering on the Centennial trucks was inspired by the lettering on historic Chevrolet trucks as well.

Celebrating the past is one thing, but, as Piszar pointed out, "You can't keep cranking out the same old notion of what pickup truck is for one hundred years. You have to adapt to the customers' needs and the needs of the times."

As this book went to print, engineers and designers were working on the next generation of Chevrolet trucks, trucks being created to marry one hundred years of experience with twenty-first–century technology for customers today and in the years to come.

"Developing an all-new truck program is a huge undertaking with literally thousands of people from across all functions," said Tim Herrick, Executive Chief Engineer for Chevrolet's next-generation trucks. "For the team, we sought out a cross-section of talents—pairing people with thirty years of truck experience with technical experts in the latest engineering, manufacturing, and design tools."

The goal is to deliver the durability and capability customers expect in a Chevrolet truck with the technological innovations that are transforming the entire automotive industry.

"The pace of innovation is accelerating at a phenomenal rate," Herrick said. "As such, you will see trucks offering levels of performance, efficiency, and connectivity that were unimaginable five or ten years ago."

Already, he pointed out, every 2016-model-year Chevrolet truck can be equipped with features such as a trailering camera-system with as many as four cameras, including one providing a rear view from the back of the trailer; smartphone projection for Apple or Android devices; a 4G LTE Internet connection; and the ability to access many vehicle features through a smartphone—such as remote-starting your truck—using the MyChevrolet app.

But even newer levels of connectivity will be available for the next-generation trucks. Truck and trailer will be able to communicate, for example, opening the possibility of checking everything from trailer tire pressures to anti-lock braking integration. Adaptive cruise control, blind-spot alert, and lane departure warning technologies are also anticipated to make driving easier and safer, with or without a trailer in tow.

BELOW: The Special Ops special-edition Silverados have ghosted side insignias and other Navy SEAL–inspired equipment. Sales of the truck benefit military families through Trident House Charities.

FOLLOWING PAGES: Then and now: vintage and brand-new Chevrolet trucks at the surf shack. Shown with a Chevy classic is a 2017 Shoreline-edition Chevrolet Colorado.

Even though the current diesel-powered Colorado provides both 30 miles per gallon and 7,700 pounds of towing capacity, the next-generation Chevrolet trucks promise enhanced fuel efficiency across the lineup by combining powertrain improvements with the use of advanced, lighter-weight materials.

While Chevrolet trucks are known to be the longest-lasting, most dependable on the road, durability validation for the next generation has been doubled. To meet that standard, the development team has accumulated more than 200 million miles in testing. That's more miles than for any vehicle program in

Chevrolet history, and—talk about "finding new roads"—nearly enough miles to have driven to Mars!

"We're going to do things in our next-generation of full-size trucks that will change the discussion and the landscape," Herrick said. "We stand on the shoulders of giants. This is the economic engine for our company. How do we refine what they've done in the past? It's more than a box on the back with people protected inside. How do you make it better? How do you integrate it better? How flexible can my architecture be to move quickly [as technology evolves]?"

BOTH: The Centennial-edition 2018 Chevrolet Silverado (left) and Colorado (right) will wear a special retro-styled Chevrolet bowtie and 100 Years badging.

The team working on the next-generation truck also realizes that while trucks are used for work and play, they also have become part of their owner's personality—"a fashion statement," as Herrick observed.

Design. Technology. Durability. Dependability. A Chevrolet truck has to offer all of that and more.

"Today's truck customers are more diverse than ever," Herrick said. "For those that use a truck for work every day, they demand uncompromised capability. For weekend warriors, they want the features and fuel economy for commuting every day, and the capability to haul all their toys on the weekend."

"For a century, Chevrolet trucks have helped millions of people around the world navigate the landscape of their lives and get the job done by lasting longer, being more durable, and offering the right level of technology and capability," said Tim Mahoney, Global Chevrolet Chief Marketing Officer.

"Chevrolet will continue to build on that strong foundation," he said, "by drawing on the innovative spirit and 'Never Give Up' determination of Louis Chevrolet to deliver even more performance and capability in its trucks for generations to come."

Acknowledgments

This book may have my name on its cover, but there were many people who contributed to its completion. I'll start with Zack Miller, publisher for the Motorbooks imprint of Quarto Publishing Group, who suggested I undertake the research and writing. Next is Monte Doran of the Chevrolet Communications team, who noted that this is the fourth book project on which we've teamed—since it's my fifth book on a GM product, he's taking credit for the other one as well!

Other GM personnel making significant contributions include Brenda Eitelman of Chevrolet Global Trademark Licensing, Greg Wallace, and especially Christo Datini of the GM Heritage Center. I should also recognize Peggy Kelly of the GM Media Archive, the group that provided the photos and advertising images included in this book.

GM engineers and marketing executives who agreed to be interviewed for the book include Anita Burke, Tim Herrick, Carl Hillenbrand, Jeff Luke, Tim Mahoney, and Sandor Piszar. Former GM staffer Scot Keller, now of the LeMay-America's Car Museum, also spoke with me.

Other GM staffers who helped set up the interviews and provided additional information and assistance include Randy Fox, Claudia Stratmann, Brian Thomas, Hugh Milne, Yeonhee Choi, Kyle Suba, Pam Flores, Miranda Spradlin, Gene Reamer, Jill Mida, Kaitlyn Hassett, and Christine Kunde.

Also contributing assistance were Charles Robertson of Equity Management, Bill Wilt, Andrew Punzal, Christie Greiner, and Voytek Orlik of Commonwealth (the Chevrolet advertising agency), Eric Pylvanainen of Pacific Communications Group, Jonathan Klinger of Hagerty, and Alyssa Bluhm of Motorbooks/Quarto.

Bibliography

BOOKS

Edsall, Larry. *Masters of Car Design*. Vercelli, Italy: White Star Publishers, 2008.

Gunnell, John. *Standard Catalog of Chevrolet Trucks*. Iola, Wisconsin: Krause Publications, 1995.

Lamm, Michael, and Dave Holls. *A Century of Automotive Style: 100 Years of American Car Design*. Stockton, California: Lamm-Morada Publishing, 1997.

Lenzke, James T., ed. *Standard Catalog of American Light-Duty Trucks*. Iola, Wisconsin: Krause Publications, 2001.

Mueller, Mike. *Chevrolet Pickups*. Minneapolis, Minnesota: Motorbooks, 2004.

PERIODICALS

Diamond, Jason. "How Bob Seger's 'Like a Rock' Defined a Generation of American Sports." Rolling Stone (September 2016): www.rollingstone.com/sports/bob-segers-like-a-rock-commercial-and-american-sports-w438146

Halpert, Julie. "Chevy's Most Enduring Advertising Campaigns: How the Ideas Took Root." Advertising Age (October 2011): www.adage.com/article/special-report-chevy-100/chevy-s-campaign-ideas-root/230682

WEBSITES

Coachbuilt
Coach builder information
www.coachbuilt.com

Deve's Technical Tetwork
Advance Design Chevrolet Trucks
www.devestechnet.com

Fourwheeler Network
www.fourwheeler.com

PickupTrucks.com
Find new & used trucks (powered by Cars.com)
www.pickuptrucks.com

TrucksPlanet.com
Trucks news, history, photo archives, PDF brochures
www.trucksplanet.com

Truck Trend Network
www.trucktrend.com

Index